FROM THE PEWS

Powerful Reflections from Key Scriptures to Grow Your Faith

MERIS HAUGHTON

FROM THE PEWS. Copyright © 2023. Meris Haughton. All Rights Reserved.

Printed in the United States of America.

No portion of this book may be reproduced, stored in a retrieval system, or transmitted in any form or by any means, except for brief quotations in printed reviews, without the prior written permission of DayeLight Publishers or Meris Haughton.

ISBN: 978-1-958443-50-7 (paperback)

All scripture quotations, unless otherwise stated, were taken from the New International Version translation. New International Version®, NIV®. Copyright © 1973, 1978, 1984 by Biblica, Inc.™ Used by permission of Zondervan. All rights reserved worldwide.

Scripture quotations marked "KJV" are taken from the Holy Bible, King James Version (Public Domain).

Scripture quotations marked (NLT) are taken from the Holy Bible, New Living Translation, copyright © 1996, 2004, 2007 by Tyndale House Foundation. Used by permission of Tyndale House Publishers, Inc., Carol Stream, Illinois 60188. All rights reserved.

Scripture quotations marked "ESV" are from the ESV Bible® (The Holy Bible, English Standard Version®), copyright © 2001 by Crossway Bibles, a publishing ministry of Good News Publishers. Used by permission. All rights reserved.

The "NASB," "NAS," "New American Standard Bible," and "New American Standard" trademarks are registered in the United States Patent and Trademark Office by The Lockman Foundation. Use of these trademarks requires the permission of The Lockman Foundation.

Scripture quotations marked TPT are from The Passion Translation®. Copyright © 2017, 2018, 2020 by Passion & Fire Ministries, Inc. Used by permission. All rights reserved. ThePassionTranslation.com.

FOREWORD

I consider it an honour to be asked to share in what I pray will be the first of several publications from the pen of our beloved in Christ, Meris. It is an understatement to profess, "Our God is an awesome God." He who, as the hymn writer enjoins, "plants His footsteps in the sea and rides upon the storm. He rolled back the waters of the mighty Red Sea. He said 'I will lead you; put your trust in Me.'"

It is true to say that *From the Pews* was born out of the leading of the Holy Spirit of God. With the advent of COVID-19 came the need to do church differently. We became acutely aware that the virtual church had become a reality, and steps were taken to bring the congregation up to speed with the use of technology. Our sister was onboard from almost the "get-go." Her numerous presentations in her work-a-world had her well poised and prepared for what would become a regular feature in her spiritual life. Her time came and she accepted without hesitation the task of leading worship, presenting a reflection or reading from the Holy Scripture. I was privy to her first presentation. She was a natural. With ease, clarity, and sincerity, she delivered a word from God for a time such as this. Her early days as a youth leader in the St. David's Church in Yallahs, St. Thomas were now being taken to the next level. They were now bearing fruit. Her deep devotion to Christ our Lord and her ability to connect with the Holy Writ would allow Meris to take challenging passages from scripture and cause a message to reach her hearers.

On examining her table of contents, it is clear that she takes a dive into this business of life. She sets out her subthemes and, beginning with her journey, she moves progressively through to the blessings of life.

I commend this work to you and invite you on a journey with our budding author. I know there are blessings awaiting all who venture on this journey with her.

In His Service,
The Reverend Father Franklyn Jackson
Pastor, Church of St. Margaret, Liguanea

ACKNOWLEDGEMENTS

My heavenly Father, thank You for placing on my heart the call to write and share these reflections. I pray that these words of my mouth and the meditations of my heart be acceptable in Thy sight. Every praise to You, my Lord.

I thank the Lord for my family, particularly my mother, Peaches, and aunts of blessed memory, Monica and Patsy, as well as my aunt, Audrey, who is still in this realm. They all guided me on my early spiritual walk, journeying with me into adulthood, and always encouraged my creativity. Moreover, I cannot leave out the positive influence of my maternal and paternal clans for modelling and shaping my spirit of love for my neighbour and serving others.

I feel blessed for my family of God, my church of St. Margaret, Liguanea family, especially Father Franklyn Jackson and the entire Evening Prayer Team for giving me a platform to grow spiritually and allowing me to be able to share From the Pews.

I am grateful for my entire tribe of influencers, including my wide circle of friends, neighbours, schoolmates, colleagues, book coach, and all my supporters who helped me breathe life into this book, my project of love.

TABLE OF CONTENTS

Foreword iii
Acknowledgements v
Introduction 11
Chapter 1: My Journey of Christian Life 13
   And He Walks With Me 14
Chapter 2: Celebrations of Life 19
   New Year's Resolution 20
   The Wedding Feast 24
   Celebrate Life, Celebrate Christ 27
   We Are Family 31
Chapter 3: Seasons of Life 37
   It's Spring Again 38
   Best Friday 41
   Easter Time 44
   The Harvest is Plentiful 48
Chapter 4: Storms of Life 53
   Hurricane Winds of Life 54
   Earth-Shattering Betrayal 58

    He Makes the Blind See 61

    Lord, Heal Our Spiritual Blindness 64

    Keep Our Eyes on Jesus 67

Chapter 5: Observances of Life 71

    Work and Pay 72

    Emancipendence of a Nation 76

    Not All Heroes Wear a Cape 80

    Old Time Christmas 84

Chapter 6: Principles of Life 89

    Faith and Forgiveness 90

    Hope and Expectation 94

    A Prayer of HOPE for Today 96

    Love Thy Neighbour 98

    The Power of Prayer 102

    Repent and Be Friends with God Again 106

    Trust and Obey 109

Chapter 7: Miracles of Life 113

    Jesus Changes Water to Wine 114

    Feed the People 118

    Spiritual Change 121

    In Sickness and in Health 125

Chapter 8: Blessings of Life 129

    He Knows My Name 130

Testify of the Goodness of God 134
Serving Others is a Blessing 137
We Are God's Messengers.. 141
The Ministrations of Women 145
I Will Follow Him.. 148
About the Author 153

INTRODUCTION

These Bible reflections began as my personal commitment to share on first Fridays and on special occasions at the live-streamed daily Evening Prayer outreach ministry introduced by my church, St. Margaret, Liguanea, as we navigated the uncertainty of the global COVID-19 pandemic. *From the Pews* is a collection of my reflections on key scriptures, that I shared based on my own experiences as a non-clerical Jamaican woman.

To my surprise, the meditations shared resulted in the deepening of my own faith and fellowship in Christ. I received positive feedback, not just from my family and friends, but also from colleagues and persons at home and aboard—who I have never met—who viewed the reflections on my church's social media platforms. They shared that the messages strengthened their own faith and prayed that I continue in my lay ministry. The feedback and words of encouragement received touched and humbled me.

I know that the Christian walk, to borrow a line from a popular reggae song, "is not an easy road." Truthfully, some of the teachings are hard to understand and harder to follow. This was as true in Biblical times—when many disciples deserted Jesus—as it is for many persons in our time.

However, being able to relate Bible stories to everyday life helped me to understand them and deepen my own faith journey. I have been inspired to write and share some of the devotional reflections to empower, encourage and strengthen you on your own Christian journey.

This book, *From the Pews,* does just that. The reflections shared cover everyday situations in life, such as celebrations, seasons, storms, observances, principles, miracles, and blessings. I invite you to use them as personal devotionals or for group Bible discussions to help you grow in your understanding and faith in Christ.

I pray that reading these reflections will bless you as they blessed me in sharing them.

CHAPTER 1

MY JOURNEY OF CHRISTIAN LIFE

"Train a child in the way he should go, and when he is old he will not turn from it" (Proverbs 22:6).

It is said that the journey of a thousand miles begins with one step. So it is with the Christian journey. However, we must remember that sometimes, as we walk, we will stumble and fall, but with God's love, we can always get back up and He will carry us through.

Reflection on John 6:60-70

And He Walks With Me

I am a born and bred country girl who grew up in the 1970s and 1980s in the small seaside town of Yallahs, St. Thomas, Jamaica. My own journey of faith started with me being baptized as a baby in the Catholic church. My mother, Peaches, who is an Anglican, and my Aunt Monica, a Roman Catholic, were my early role models of Christian living and giving. Like many of my generation, on Sundays I would go to church and attend Sunday school. This was at St. David's Anglican Church where I also received my confirmation as a pre-teen.

As I grew older, I became active in our church's youth ministry and was part of the youth group of the Anglican, Catholic, and Methodist church. You see, this was pre-internet and multiple television stations, so there was not much else to do in the country, if you don't count going to the beach, playing games, climbing trees, and having fun with my many siblings, cousins, and friends. However, being involved in activities at all these churches gave me an appreciation for different Christian denominations, so thankfully, I do not have the hang-ups about different churches as some persons do.

My Christian journey also led me to be involved in service clubs and to embrace the values of Mercy Charism of dignity, excellence, justice, service, and stewardship while in high school at the Alpha Academy. This is an all-girl's school operated by the Catholic church.

Sadly, my journey took a different turn in 1991, around the time my father, who was just fifty-three, died. I was twenty-two. Alas, I began to drift away from church. You see, I had recently finished college, started to work, and told myself I had to live life to the fullest, as no one knows what tomorrow brings. I guess it was my own "eat, drink and be merry" period. My direction shifted to going to nightclubs, reggae shows, and soca sessions. As a good friend of mine used to say, "Every pan knock, I was there."

Much to my mother's distress, I became part of what my now pastor and friend call the "hatch, match, and dispatch" group. I only went to church for baptisms, weddings, and funerals. Therefore, I understand when young people stray from church. So, don't give them a hard time, as thankfully, they usually continue to serve and eventually return.

Now, don't get me wrong, I was still very service-oriented, continuing to do good deeds. I was active—and still am—in a Kiwanis Club and serving my Alma Mater. However, the Bible tells us that doing good works alone is not enough, "For it is by grace you have been saved, through faith… not by works." (Ephesians 2:8-9). We need to have a personal relationship with Christ. We must walk with Him and for Him.

Meris Haughton

Although I did not have a prodigal son, rock-bottom experience, I knew something was missing. I could not quite put my finger on it, but there was a void. I did not feel like I was being purposeful. I felt like I was just going through the motions.

I would periodically visit the Church of St. Margaret, Liguanea, as I had relocated to the city. My turning point started in 1997. I attended a special church service arranged for our inaugural Bogle Family reunion, celebrating our rich heritage and family togetherness. The message delivered by the pastor was on the importance of not just our family but, more importantly, the family of God. It stuck with me. The following year, when I turned thirty, I remember making a conscious decision to start going back to church.

Thankfully, I never forgot my Christian upbringing. I remembered that Jesus is the answer and slowly began to walk with Christ again. I started going back to church more regularly and becoming involved in church organisations and activities, and reading the Bible more consistently. In addition, more importantly, again having a personal relationship with Christ Jesus and doing daily devotions.

The good news is that there are others like me who walk away for a while and return to Jesus. We should always encourage others and help them find their way back to Christ. We have to help them along the way in their walk. Sadly, some leave and never return. Others, like the Apostle

Peter, remain steadfast followers and leaders in their own right.

However, even those of us who remain with or return to Christ are tested. Walking with Christ does not mean we will not have moments when we struggle. Like many other persons, I too face struggles. One of the biggest struggles I faced was in 2018 when I went from the high of a weeklong celebration for my 50th birthday, to—just a week later—the low of the news that my mother's cancer was back with a bang. The next few months, from her sickness to her earthly exit, were an emotional and physical rollercoaster. However, through it all, I remained rooted and grounded in Christ. I found strength in prayer, the tremendous support of my church, and witnessing my mom's continued faith in the face of fear. Besides, I am forever grateful for the many earth angels and my own village people who walked with me, and still do.

Friends, we never walk alone. Sure, there will be moments when we feel we cannot take another step and think that Christ has deserted us. However, it is at these times that Christ will lift us up and carry us along through the support of family, friends, and faith.

So, I urge you to build up your stamina for the hills and valleys of your own Christian journey by reading the Word daily, praying without ceasing, deepening your understanding through Bible study, fellowshipping in church, and giving of your talent, time, and treasure to your church, service organisations and others. Discipleship or following Christ is something we have to do intentionally.

Remember, Jesus IS the answer. So, stay the course, my friend, and walk in faith as Christ walks with us.

CHAPTER 2

CELEBRATIONS OF LIFE

"Be cheerful with joyous celebration in every season of life. Let your joy overflow!" (Philippians 4:4 – TPT).

In our life, as it was in biblical times, there is so much to celebrate. As children of God, we should therefore not be afraid to celebrate those special moments and anniversaries, as even Christ Himself celebrated with His family and friends. Let us celebrate; just make sure that Christ is invited to the party.

Reflection of John 6:30-33, 48-51

New Year's Resolution

It is fascinating to note that bread has been a part of the human diet for over 30,000 years.

I remember when I was younger, on Fridays, my parents used to stop and buy the tastiest freshly baked white hard dough bread from a bakery on the outskirts of the city at Harbour View Shopping Centre. While on the drive home to Yallahs in the country, my tribe of siblings and cousins would take one of the hot breads, break it, dip it in butter we had bought at the grocery store, and eat it. My mouth is watering just thinking about it.

Nowadays, there are so many other bread options; sesame seed, whole wheat, natural bran, French bread, garlic bread, you name it, they bake it. Bread is one of those carbs that many persons just cannot resist.

In biblical times, bread was also very popular. A quick Google search says there are almost 500 references to bread in the Bible, from Genesis to Revelation. It is therefore understandable that Jesus used this simple staple to make a point about Himself. Yes, my friend, Jesus is the best thing since slice bread, as noted in the biblical story "***Jesus the Bread of Life.***"

That is right; bread is nourishment for the body, but *Jesus offers spiritual bread that feeds our souls*. It brings our spirit to life and offers a way to salvation. It is why each time persons take Holy Communion, they remember the Last Supper when Jesus took the unleavened bread, broke it, and gave it to His disciples to symbolize His broken body and His death on the cross on our behalf.

The bread of life that Jesus represents will never go stale or mildewed. This kind will not make us put on weight or overload us with carbs. What it will do is give us life in this world and the next. My late sister, Holly, who died unexpectedly at age fifty-two, fed on this bread while she was here on this earth, and we believe that it will preserve her and other believers into the next.

Therefore, whenever we face a brand-new year, or at any time really, with uncertainties, we too should remember that Christ gives us hope for a brighter tomorrow, if we feed on Him and His Word.

I therefore challenge persons to recommit themselves to Christ, the bread of life, by considering these five resolutions for a New Year or a new life in Christ:

1. **To diet more on the Word of God**: We need to feed on the Word and to have a balanced diet of going to church regularly, reading the Bible daily and participating in Bible study and fellowship groups.

2. **To exercise daily love for our neighbours**: Sadly, our society has become very hostile. We therefore need to do our part to being kinder and gentler to one another. Get involved in outreach activities in your communities. Let us practice the "each one, help one" principle.

3. **To spend more time breaking bread together and in fellowship with others**: Even in the face of several transmissible viruses and the busyness of life, we need to remain social, even if we are physically distant. Pay special attention to the elderly, who are often lonely. Phone, video call, or message someone you have not spoken to for a while. Keep in touch with family and friends today as tomorrow may be too late.

4. **To give more to the church and the less fortunate**: The need is great, especially in these difficult times. So, let us do more to help each other. Most churches have a feeding programme, or a can-drive, so why not walk with a can of food to donate each time you go to church. Moreover, believe me, it does not take much to make others happy; you can simply share a sandwich with them.

5. **To commit to spreading the Word of God**: It does not make sense we fatten ourselves while others starve for the truth. In the words of that old spiritual song, "Go tell it on the mountain that Jesus Christ is

Lord." Try telling others about Christ where you work and play. In addition, do not just say it, but show it too.

So, no matter what your own resolutions are, just remember that in John 6:51, Jesus said, *"I am the living bread which came down from heaven, if anyone eats of this bread, he will live for ever."*

Let us taste and see the possibilities for the New Year and beyond, that through Christ, we can have life and have it more abundantly.

Reflection of Matthew 22:1-14

The Wedding Feast

The *Parable of the Wedding Banquet* is a well-known one drawing on the culture of a wedding feast. This is a custom that many Jamaicans can identify with, as traditionally, we like to put on a grand spread, killing not just the fattened calf, but the fattened pig, goat, chicken, fish, lobster, you name it. Of course, inviting all and sundry to attend.

Given the size and closeness of my own family, it wasn't surprising when my mom would tell us stories of her wedding being a small carnival with dozens of families and friends first going to the church, then the reception, which went on from morning into the night with lots of food, drink, and music. Our family loves a good party. Unfortunately, there are very few pictures after midway through the reception as the photographer was busy partaking of other "spirits," but that is another story.

The COVID-19 pandemic temporarily put the brakes on such large celebrations. It has taught us to be more judicious about who we choose to invite. I even know of persons who put off their wedding feast during COVID-19. You see, for the first two years of the pandemic, COVID-19 protocols were the deciding factor of the maximum number of persons who could attend a wedding in person. It moved from zero when we had full lockdown to 15, to 20, to 30, to 50 and then to 100, before finally returning to normal.

In the biblical wedding feast in the parable, those first invited refused to come. Clearly, this was not a Jamaican country wedding, as some persons cannot resist going, whether or not they have an invitation. In the parable, the servants then went to the street corners and invited to the banquet anyone they could find. The banquet that represents the kingdom of God has no limit. This heavenly feast is open to the rich and the poor, to the educated and the illiterate, to the young and the old, to males and females, to Christians and non-Christians; in fact, ALL ARE INVITED.

The parable shows us that the teachings of Christ and the Kingdom of God are universal and, therefore, for everyone. My household, at times, is testimony to that. There are times when there is an Anglican, a Roman Catholic, and an Adventist under the same roof. But guess what? We all serve one God.

In Matthew 22:14, it tells us that *"For many are invited."* Nevertheless, we must also recognize the proviso that says, *"but few are chosen."* The truth is, friend, Jesus comes for one; He comes for all. But, sadly, not all will heed the call. Not all will follow the teachings, so not all will get in.

It is our responsibility to be discerning to follow the path of Christ, hear the words of scriptures, and not blindly follow the roadmap or GPS of man. Unfortunately, we have seen in recent times where false prophets and even false doctrines have led persons astray.

As Judy Mowatt, one of Jamaica's reggae icons, sang, "Many are called, but few are chosen. You've got to be aware of the wolf in sheep clothing."

This is why it is important to answer the call, and to live a life of purpose and one full of love.

When my younger sister died, after a one-month battle with cancer, it confirmed the principle of purpose for me. Understandably, it saddened and pained me. However, at the same time, I was happy when I thought of how she lived her life as a shining example of answering God's call. She found her purpose in teaching and displayed a heart of gold in adopting her beautiful daughter, who is our family's treasure. Even more than that, she had a passion for helping others, especially children. That is why it was a perfect fit for her to become the Director of the Foster Care Programme at Family Life Ministries. I have no doubt in my mind that based on how she lived her life with such purpose, that she would be among those chosen to enter the Kingdom of God.

While we have time, it is for us to be like Christ or to follow the example of my sister, and love God and our neighbour as ourselves. I encourage you to do your part to live a purpose-filled and loving life, to not just be called by God but, more importantly, to fulfil the promise to be chosen. Do it today, as tomorrow may be too late.

Reflection of Mark 14:1-11

Celebrate Life, Celebrate Christ

August 25 is my birthday, and as my family and friends know, I usually start celebrating on August 1 and do something special to mark the actual day.

I had a BIG celebration in 2018 when I turned fifty. It was extra special, not just because I was observing a milestone, but because my mom, who was seriously ill, was there to share it with me. I actually considered aborting the festivities, but my mom was against it. She truly believed in celebrating life, as tomorrow may never come.

Growing up, my family took observing special dates and celebrating milestones very seriously. We would get together for any and everything; birthdays, graduations, passing exams, reunions, births, deaths, you name it. As we say in Jamaica, if a baby "buss" teeth (meaning a baby begins to grow teeth), we had a celebration.

Celebrations are important. The backdrop to Mark 14:1-11 was during the time of the religious observance of ***Passover and the Festival of the Unleavened Bread***. Besides, throughout the New Testament, we see many examples of Jesus participating in other social and religious festivities of the time. I guess if it was in our time, He would go to gospel concerts or hang out on the corner eating Jamaican jerk chicken, drinking something, and reasoning with the guys.

However, on this occasion, Jesus was chilling in the home of Simon the Leper. To honour Him, a woman took a bottle of expensive perfume and poured it on Jesus' head. Can you imagine that? He must have reeked of it. But while the others around started to quarrel with the lady for wasting the perfume, complaining that it could have been sold and the money given to the poor, Jesus immediately shut them down, then used the incident as a teaching moment.

In Mark 14:7, Jesus told the gathering, *"The poor you will always have with you, and you can help them any time you want. But you will not always have me."*

This reminds me of when I told a church sister of my plans to have a big bash for my 50th birthday. She asked me why I was wasting money on a party and suggested that instead I should donate the money to the poor. I calmly told her I would only turn fifty once. Not to mention that it was my money, but if it made her feel better, I had asked guests to donate to my church in lieu of a gift.

But, seriously, friend, it is a reality we face that the poor will always be with us. Sadly, today, poverty is on the rise, not just in Jamaica but worldwide, and it is compounded by several global crises.

From the Pews

We are called to do what we can for others. It does not have to be something grand. It may be as simple as saying a kind word to someone; donating a tin or two from your pantry to the poor. Giving a "smalls" to the person at the stoplight or to someone who knocks at your door. You could sponsor a child for back-to-school. Since I turned fifty, I have made it a point to gift a special donation to my church on my birthday to mark the number of years I have been on earth.

As Jesus told the disciples in Mark 14:8, in reference to the woman's kindness, *"she did what she could."* Moreover, so should we. Acts 20:35 teaches that, *"It is more blessed to give than to receive."*

The principle of giving in Proverbs 11:25 suggests that when we are generous with others, we are likely to receive generosity as well. That is not to say we should give expecting something in return. Instead, we should give to help others in loving response to God's instruction to do so. As Jesus was with the woman in the passage, our giving will please God.

While we should always do what we can for the poor, there is nothing wrong with balancing that with our own celebrations and festivities marking important dates. Let us however remember to have God in the centre of all we do.

That is why, as I celebrate each year, I choose to share with others and to thank God for my many blessings. So, friend,

Meris Haughton

celebrate your life, *"Eat, drink and be merry, as tomorrow we die." (Ecclesiastes 8:15).*

Reflection of John 15:1-17

We Are Family

Jesus said to His disciples in John 15:12, *"My command is this: Love each other as I have loved you."* This is a command that transcends time and is as true today as it was in biblical times. Moreover, it is equally a command to us individually, as it is to us as a family.

The story in John 15:1-17 of ***The Vine and the Branches*** reminds me how important the roots of my family are to me. I love my family, and I have no doubt my family loves me. I am therefore thankful that my family has a tradition of having a big reunion every four years. We always start our weekend family celebration in worship by showing our love for God and our love for family.

For me, family and love are synonymous. That is how my family was socialised. From "wi yeye deh a wi knee" (for non-Jamaicans, that means when we were knee high or little), we were taught to look out for each other and share whatever we had.

While growing up, I can remember there were always extra persons at our dinner table, especially on Sundays and during holidays. Sometimes, it was like feeding the five thousand. However, my mom used to smile and say, "Bless it, and it will stretch it." And, guess what? She was right; there was always enough.

Family is also at the centre of God's plan for the happiness and progress of His children. The Holy Bible teaches that God established families from the very beginning when He created Adam and Eve as the first family (see Genesis 1). In addition, there are many biblical verses about the strength of family in the Old and New Testaments. Mind you, it also shows the human weakness and reality of all families, showing the good, the bad, and the ugly.

There are stories of disobedience, greed, betrayal, jealousy, hatred, and other negatives. There is Cain killing Abel; Jacob taking Esau's blessing from their father, Isaac, by scamming, costing him his birthright; and many other such stories.

However, thanks be to God, it also teaches us the strength of sacrifice, unconditional love, helping one another, and the recipe to having a loving, happy family. There is the story of the father joyfully welcoming home the prodigal son, even after he had squandered his inheritance. There is that great love story of Joseph and Mary. Think about it. When Joseph thought Mary had cheated on him and had given him "bun," as we say in Jamaica, he never made a stink about it. He had planned to annul their marriage quietly. However, after the angel had a talk with him, he, as we say in Jamaica, wore his "jacket" with pride and raised Jesus as his own with unconditional love.

From the Pews

As Jesus explained in John 15:13, *"Greater love has no one than this: to lay down one's life for one's friends."* For me, that means family.

The Bible really has some very exciting stories. No wonder it is a bestseller. My own family is full of so much excitement and drama. I often tell people that many in our family do not even bother to watch soap operas. Although there were some very popular ones when I was younger, like The Bold and Beautiful, The Young and the Restless, Days of Our Lives, Dallas, and recent favourites like Abbot Elementary or the Bridgeton's. In fact, right in my family there are so many stories, we could probably write and produce our own soap opera. We could call it, The Bright and the Bogles. Thankfully, in spite of all the drama, our family is also full of so much rich history; sharing, caring, fun, togetherness, and, above all, LOVE.

Nevertheless, even though in the midst of life there is death, never forget that in the midst of death, there is LIFE and LOVE.

Family means everything. I believe our Bogle Family is especially blessed as, through the many generations, the lines are often blurred as sometimes we are not too sure who is a brother, sister, aunt, cousin or friend. So blurred are these lines that for years, whenever I would visit my aunt's church, I couldn't convince two little old ladies there that I was her niece and not her daughter. They would even ask me for my cousin; that was me. I gave up after a while and just went with their story.

Moreover, I think every family in every generation has similar stories of blurred lines, of sister/cousins or aunty/mother. I know many in my own family consider all the younger nieces, nephews, and cousins, whether by birth or adoption, as our own children.

That is why sometimes when I share family stories with other people, they ask me, "How many aunts and cousins you one have?" It doesn't matter as we are one big family, equally proud of and loving each other as our own.

What is love? In 1 Corinthians 13:4-8, it tells us that, *"Love is patient, love is kind. It does not envy, it does not boast, it is not proud. It is not rude, it is not self-seeking, it is not easily angered, it keeps no record of wrongs. Love does not delight in evil but rejoices with the truth. It always protects, always trusts, always hopes, and always perseveres. Love never fails..."*

Yes, my family truly believes that all we need is LOVE. However, we should not take this love for granted and should often tell our family members, "I love you."

We honour God and our ancestors when we gather for family celebrations in worship and love. Moreover, it doesn't really matter the denomination to which we belong. Paul Bogle, our famous ancestor and one of Jamaica's national hero, was a Baptist deacon. Some of my families are Anglicans, Catholics, Adventists, and some are even non-denominational. What is important is that we know who we are and whose we are. We are all God's children, even if we praise God and show our faith in many different ways.

We look forward to one of my aunts, who is really a cousin, posting a daily scripture passage and meditation in our family WhatsApp group. I have heard one of my cousins, Dennis, preaching like the Apostle Paul. Some of the younger ones used to sing or play musical instruments or dance in church. In addition, personally, since June 2020, during the height of COVID-19, I made a commitment to lead evening prayer on first Fridays at my church. Moreover, I know that there are other ways that we share our faith.

Equally important is that others should know we are a strong family and Christians by our love. I therefore end as I started and remind us as Jesus repeated His command to His disciples in John 15:17, *"Love each other."*

CHAPTER 3

SEASONS OF LIFE

"There is a time for everything, and a season for every activity under heaven." (Ecclesiastes 3:1).

We go through many seasons throughout our lives. There are seasons of the calendar, and there are liturgical seasons. However, no matter the season, God is in control.

The following reflections look at how we can navigate these seasons with Christ by our side.

Reflection of Luke 8:1-15

It's Spring Again

"There is a time to plant and a time to harvest." (Ecclesiastes 3:2 – NLT).

As a born and bred country girl, who grew up on a small farm, I have always been drawn to the *Parable of the Sower* in Luke 8:1-15. It is a well-known parable that resonates with many Jamaicans. However, clearly, it also resonated with the gospel writers as three of the four gospels record an account of it. But what does it mean? From Jesus' explanation to the disciples in Luke 8:11-15, the seed represents the gospel, the sower represents anyone who proclaims it, and the various soils represent people's responses to it. This is the truth yesterday, today and tomorrow.

Coincidentally, I remember watching a movie on Netflix titled "All Saints." When I watched it, I actually thought of this Bible story. It is a true story of a salesman turned Anglican Priest who was appointed to oversee the closure of a rural church in Tennessee, USA. It was up for sale due to low membership and high debts. To cut a long story short, the minister requested and got a reprieve. His plan was to grow crops on the church lands to raise funds to pay off the mortgage. That way, the church, which was also providing shelter to several Asian refugees, would not have to close.

However, his farm idea, like many things in life, did not go according to plan. Alas, due to a storm, some of the crops washed away before he could reap everything.

It may sound like a sad story, but thanks be to God, there was a silver lining behind the storm clouds. You see, the seeds sown bore unexpected fruits. As they sowed the seeds on the farm, they also sowed the seed of the gospel. As the crops grew, so did the church membership. Another amazing thing happened. An entire community came together to help in the cause. In the end, they saved the church and the refugees.

I share this story because, as Jesus said, as sowers, we have to understand that there are different soils representing various hearts, but there is always some good. Just to be clear, we can preach like Paul the apostle, but not everybody will hear and understand or even want to hear. Some will heed for a while but quickly lose interest. Others will follow, but their many distractions will get in the way. Thankfully, some will grow in Christ and bear fruit.

Added to that, any farmer will tell you that it is the plants that grow in the well-prepared soil that is properly tended that will likely bear fruit, even if they go through the challenges of nature. Flood rains may cause some farmers to lose their crops, but because of their passion, some never stop sowing. It should be the same for us. We should take a page out of the farmer's book and sow the gospel without ceasing. We are called to never stop sowing the Word of God.

Like a good farmer, before we even plant the seeds, we have to prepare the soil. We also have to tend the plants; that is why we need to prepare through studying the Bible, worshipping together, and praying without ceasing. We must also spread the seed of the gospel, not just by our words, but also, more importantly, by our deeds. We should share our time, treasure, and talent, helping others, doing good and, above all, having a personal relationship with God.

We are also called to be good soil and prepare ourselves and others to face the storms and hardships of life that we will undoubtedly face. We all face challenges, perhaps with relationships, death, sickness, loss of a job, crime and just life. But, by the grace of God, if we continue to grow in faith, we will surely reap the fruit of the spirit, that is, love, joy, peace, patience, kindness, goodness, faithfulness, gentleness, self-control (see Galatians 5:22-23).

Ask yourself these questions: *Are you a sower? Are you planting seeds? What kind of soil are you?*

I encourage you to keep being a farmer in God's garden. Go forth and plant the seeds of the gospel, and I guarantee that some will fall on good soil and bear fruit.

Remember, if we do not sow, we cannot reap.

Reflection of John 19:38-42

Best Friday

John 19:38-42 gives an account of ***The Burial of Jesus***. This story, as you would imagine, was so important to the followers of Christ that all four gospels carry it. Truthfully, there are some nuances in these various accounts.

Case in point, in John 19:38-39, it says Nicodemus accompanied Joseph of Arimathea, who was secretly a disciple of Jesus, to request the body of Jesus. It says they wrapped Jesus in spices and strips of linen in accordance with the Jewish burial custom. They laid Him in a new tomb nearby, as it was the Jewish day of preparation.

In Matthew 27:57-61 we again see Joseph, described as a rich man who had become a disciple of Jesus, going to Pilate to ask for the body. In Matthew 27:59-60, we read that he wrapped the body in clean linen and placed it in his own tomb cut from rock and rolled a big stone at the entrance. Here, too, we read of the Marys sitting across from the tomb.

In Mark 15:42-47, we are told that Joseph, a prominent member of the council, who was himself waiting on the Kingdom of God, went boldly to Pilate to ask for the body of Jesus. We are told that Pilate, having confirmed that Jesus was dead, gave the body to Joseph, who bought linen, wrapped Jesus in it, placed the body in a tomb cut from rock, and rolled a stone against the entrance. We again read that Mary Magdalene and Mary, the mother of Joses, saw where He was laid.

In Luke 23:50-56, we read that Joseph was a member of the council, but he did not consent to their decision and action. With the permission of Pilate, he took the body, wrapped it in linen and placed it in a tomb cut from rock. It was Preparation Day, and Sabbath was about to begin. We again see the women featured and that they went home to prepare spices and perfumes, but they rested on the Sabbath in obedience to the commandment.

Though there are slight differences in the four gospels, what is agreed upon is that it was approaching the Sabbath (known as Preparation Day), and Joseph of Arimathea requested Jesus' body from Pilate. The body was wrapped in linen, placed in a tomb, and a big stone rolled across the entrance. In short, without a doubt, Christ died and was buried.

As a fulfilment of scripture, the story of the death and burial of Jesus is just as important to followers of Christ today as it was in yesteryear. Without a death and a burial, there could not be a resurrection.

In this modern era, we as Christians could say TGFF: Thank God for Friday; Good Friday, that is.

Yes, we thank God for the gift of His Son, born to be sacrificed on the cross to save all of us. This gift of love is summed up in John 3:16, *"God so loved the world that He gave His one and only Son, that whoever believes in him shall not perish but have eternal life."*

The gift is even more special when you think of the horror that Christ, an innocent man, went through for a sinful people then and now. Just imagine the pain and suffering He endured. The horror of the crucifixion has also been brought to the big screen in graphic details in films like the *Passion of Christ*.

Yes, Good Friday is truly good because Christ demonstrated the greatest love of all. He laid down His life to purchase our pardon on that fateful Friday.

A quick Google search shows that Good Friday has had other names throughout history by different people. There is Great Friday in Greek liturgy, Long Friday by Anglo Saxons, Holy Friday, God's Friday, and Black Friday. However, Good Friday, by any other name, is just as blessed.

Whenever we observe Good Friday, let us never forget that without a Good Friday, there would be no Easter Sunday when the glory of the Lord was seen, making it Best Sunday. It is the fulfilment of prophecy and is central to our Christian belief that Christ has died, Christ is Risen, Christ will come again.

Reflection of John 14:15-31

Easter Time

John 14:15-31 is entitled in some versions of the Bible as ***Jesus Promises the Holy Spirit.*** This happened at a time that coincided with what we refer to as Easter in our time.

There are some Easter traditions that are at the top of the list for many Jamaicans. There is the eating of fried fish and festival or the good old hard dough bread on Good Friday, and having as much bun and cheese as your heart desires. Of course, there is the tradition of all and sundry going to church on Easter Sunday, decked out in their finest, not to mention the women in their Easter hats. Some persons go to the beach or parties over the Easter weekend. I remember when I was growing up, flying kites was a favourite pastime on Easter Monday, which actually grew into an Annual Kite Festival. But Easter is much more than that. Let us not forget that the reason for the season is Christ Himself.

Yes, friend, in the Christian community, the Friday is known as Good Friday. This is when we commemorate the fateful day that Christ, out of love for humanity, gave His life upon the cross for all of us. If we think about it, I guess we could actually consider it a great Friday, as it was the greatest gift of all. Christ told His disciples in John 15:13 that, *"Greater love has no one than this, that he lay down his life for his friends."*

Then came Better Saturday. In our time, many of us keep vigil and recreate the wait for the promise of Christ rising from the dead, as did His disciples over 2000 years ago. Thankfully, we only have to imagine the anxiety and fear that His followers must have experienced then, as we have the benefit of knowing the outcome.

Then there is Best Sunday, when we, as followers of Christ, glory in His resurrection on the third day as we celebrate Easter Sunday. I can only imagine the joy of His disciples on that fateful resurrection Sunday when the promise of Christ became a reality. We too share in that joy in our Easter celebrations. In most traditional churches, the Easter celebration is rich with colourful flowers, songs of praise, and churchgoers dressed in bright colours. I must admit, I love these Easter church traditions. However, the only true way to celebrate and honour Christ is to be more like Him.

Jesus said in John 14:15, *"If you love me, you'll obey what I command."* The summary of these commands is *"Love one another as He has loved us."* We do not need any other clues on the ideal celebration of Easter time or any other time.

Throughout the New Testament, Jesus taught and showed His disciples and followers many examples of His love for others. He fed the poor, associated with outcasts, had compassion for the downtrodden, healed the sick, blessed little children, and did so much more.

We must therefore practice these things in big and small ways as we are called to show kindness and love for those we meet, not just our family and friends. I know it is not easy, friend, but the season of Easter and Christ's call for us to keep His commands remind me of that ditty we learned years ago: *Good, better, best, never let it rest until your good becomes better and your better best.* It is the same with following the teachings of Christ, which is simply to LOVE. It is something we have to practice, practice, and practice some more until we are good, better, best.

We CHOOSE to honour God every time we show love. Moreover, although Christ is risen and no longer with us in body, He has not left us alone. We do not have to fend for ourselves. In John 14:26, He told the disciples, *"But the Counselor, the Holy Spirit, whom the Father will send in my name, will teach you all things and will remind you of everything I have said to you."* It is the same message He has for us today.

Therefore, you see, we have the Holy Spirit to guide us and help us to bear the fruit of the Spirit, that is, love, joy, peace, patience, kindness, goodness, faithfulness, gentleness, self-control. These are moral virtues, all packaged in one super fruit, that we must all work to show and live according to Christ.

From the Pews

I pray that the Holy Spirit rest on me, and on you, and guide us on our walk to be like Christ. Let Him remind us that no matter what we are going through, the risen Christ is still with us.

May I remind you of what Christ wished for His disciples; indeed, He wishes for us all: *"Peace I leave with you; my peace I give you. I do not give to you as the world gives. Do not let your hearts be troubled and do not be afraid." (John 14:27)*.

Remember, Christ is risen. He is risen indeed. Alleluia!

Reflection of Matthew 9:35-38

The Harvest is Plentiful

"There's a time to plant, and a time to pluck up what is planted." (Ecclesiastes 3:2).

"Jesus said to His disciples, 'The harvest is plentiful, but the labourers are few; therefore, pray earnestly to the Lord of the harvest to send out labourers into his harvest.'" (*Matthew 9:37-38*). Christ uses this analogy in the story **The Workers are Few** to highlight the fact that there are many persons who need to be cared for, many rights to be wronged, many who need to be showered with love, and many who need to know and be brought to God. On the other hand, it demonstrates that there are too few persons to love and care for others and share the Word of God. However, it also brings to my mind the age-old 80/20 rule, where 80% of the work is done by 20% of persons. This is true in the workplace, in service organisations, schools and, yes, even in churches.

The symbolic meaning of harvest in Scripture encompasses two main areas: God's provision for us and God's blessing for others. While we celebrate a harvest season just once a year, we experience the spirit of harvest all the time. Therefore, we need to be planting year-round so we can reap always.

From the Pews

As I consider the harvest season, I cannot help thinking of Jamaica's programme that promotes, "Eat what you grow and grow what you eat." This aims to reposition the Jamaican Agricultural Sector through a process of integrated rural development as well as to develop a programme of sustainable food security. Strategically, the programme has several elements to engage a wide cross-section of persons and organisations, such as youth, churches, farmers, and householders.

However, more importantly, it also made me think that, as Christians, we should teach what we know and know what we teach. You see, just as labourers in the harvest are called to plant to promote our nation's food security, as Christians, we are called to sow the gospel to promote our nation's spiritual security.

I love to garden. I guess it is the country girl in me. So recently, I decided to redo my backyard garden to make it a semi-edible garden. Therefore, I have planted fruits, vegetables, and herbs. This was intentional to do my small part to eat what I grow and grow what I eat.

Similarly, I have been intentional in redoing my spiritual garden. I therefore did a Cursillo programme. Cursillo is a short, intense course in Christianity. It is also a movement that focuses on showing lay people how to become effective Christian leaders over the course of a three-day weekend, with a fourth day of renewal and growth for the rest of our lives. I saw it as an opportunity for new seeds of the Word to be planted in me so that I can grow in the spirit and become a better sower too. This would, in turn, make me a better labourer in God's vineyard.

Moreover, believe me, friend, we can all be sowers of the Word. It does not have to be from a pulpit but, like for me, it can be from the pews. It can also be in our home, neighbourhood, office, and even in our social circle. So, speak our truth.

It is not just what we say but also what we do. We sow seeds by how we live our lives and how we love one another. As labourers, we need to care for others, love our neighbours, give to the poor, and stand up for justice and peace. In short, we need to "liv gud" (live good), as is being promoted in Jamaica.

Nevertheless, similar to what every farmer knows, not every seed will grow. As sowers of the Word of God, we should recognise that not all our seeds of the gospel will properly take root. Difficult as it may be to accept, we are not responsible for another person's heart and soul. People have free will. To put it more plainly, the condition of a person's heart towards the Word of God is not on us; it is up to them.

We are mere labourers, so let God handle the rest. Therefore, labour on. In 1 Corinthians 3:6, Paul says, *"I planted the seed, Apollos watered it, but God made it grow."*

So, I invite you to be a labourer to *"Honor the Lord with your wealth and with the first fruits of all your produce." (Proverbs 3:9).*

Yes, friend, as spiritual planters, we need to pray without ceasing now more than ever, that our labour yields a bounty of the fruit of the Spirit: love, joy, peace, patience, kindness, goodness, faithfulness, gentleness, self-control (see Galatians 5:22-23).

I truly believe that together, we can make this world a better place. We can ALL be labourers in God's fields. It would certainly make harvesting easier, as many hands and voices do make the work lighter. So, let us plant a seed, make a friend, be a friend, and bring a friend to Christ. De Colores.

CHAPTER 4

STORMS OF LIFE

"He stilled the storm to a whisper; the waves of the sea were hushed." (Psalm 107:29).

We all face storms of life at some point in our lives. These storms, literal or symbolic, flood our lives, sometimes threatening to drown us.

These reflections in this chapter remind us that God is a constant comfort during hard times. He can calm the storms in our lives, as well as help us weather the storms.

Reflection of Mark 4:35-41

Hurricane Winds of Life

In the well-known story of *Jesus Calming the Storm*, it tells of Jesus sleeping while the disciples tried to deal with a furious squall that threatened to capsize their boat. Even though they were seasoned fishermen, they were alarmed to the point of frantically awakening Jesus and asking if He did not care that they were perishing.

This reminds me of an experience in 1988 when Hurricane Gilbert hit Jamaica. At the time, my family was still living on the eastern side of the island in Yallahs, St. Thomas. With St. Thomas being in the path of the Category 4 storm, I am sure you can imagine how terrifying it was as the howling winds actually shook the roof of our house. My mom, who was getting increasingly frantic, awakened my father and asked him how he could be sleeping in the midst of the storm. Of course, my dad could not tell the wind to hush, but he told my mom to calm down and go pray—something we all have to be reminded about sometimes. Thank God, our roof survived. Many of our neighbours were not so lucky. Nevertheless, with the help of others, they survived.

In our time and in our lives, we have seen or faced storms of one kind or another. These sometimes cause us to ask, "Where is God?" Or we ask, "Why would God let this happen?" There is nowhere in the Bible that it says following God means you will not face storms. Think about it. Joseph's own brothers sold him into slavery. Moses wandered around in the wilderness for forty years, and Jesus was persecuted and crucified. Nevertheless, they all kept their faith, and their storms served a purpose to help and save others.

On a global scale, one of the biggest storms of the 21st century was the COVID-19 pandemic. But even a storm as big as that was not insurmountable. Many countries banded together to find and share a cure. However, the world needs to take some personal responsibility and allow Christ into the boat.

Currently, there are several political storms happening across the continents that are like tsunamis. There is the Russia—Ukraine war, conflicts in Africa, bombing in the Middle East, and many other strifes. I pray that the world leaders can ride the waves and work together with the belief that Christ will calm even those storms.

On the national scene, we have literally faced many storms, including hurricanes and other weather systems. Some storms come with such an intensity that they are frightening and have a devastating aftermath that takes us a while to recover. We faced many such storms and will continue to face others. Nevertheless, they too shall pass.

Individually, too, we are faced with sudden storms in one way or another. It could be a loved one diagnosed with a chronic or terminal illness, the sudden loss of a job, a major accident, the death of a close family member, a shocking death of a colleague, or a myriad of other challenges. These sudden events sometimes make us feel like we are drowning.

However, with Jesus Christ in our boat, as the world-renowned Reggae Icon Bob Marley said, "None of them can stop the time." Jesus is our lifeline. Once we hold on to Him, no matter the outcome, we will not perish. Never forget, Christ has already saved us by dying for us.

We should also follow the flow of Apostle Paul, who shared the secret of facing storms. Moreover, although he personally faced many, he was firm in his conviction that no matter what, he could make it through with Christ. In Philippians 4:13, he wrote, *"I can do all things through Christ, who gives me strength."* This is a mantra I have adopted as my own.

If we remember that Christ is with us, even in the midst of a storm, we will be able to go through that storm. Let us therefore look for the bright side in our storms. Never forget that the sun will come out tomorrow, and there is always a rainbow after the storm.

Friend, do not panic in the face of a storm. As Jesus said to the disciples then, He is still saying to us today, "There is no need to be afraid." He instead implores us to have faith. As my mom said in the midst of her own health storm, "Don't tell God how big your storm is; tell the storm how big your God is."

Reflection: Matthew 26:47-56

Earth-Shattering Betrayal

Betrayal in personal relationships refers to the violation of your trust by someone close to you. Being on the receiving end can be earth-shattering, even rocking your world like an earthquake. Throughout history, there have been several well-known stories of betrayal.

"Et tu Brute" is a famous line from the Shakespearean play *Julius Caesar*. It marks the point when Emperor Julius Caesar recognises that his friend, Brutus, is actually one of the assassins stabbing him to death.

Then there is Benedict Arnold, an infamous traitor in American history, whose name is synonymous with treason and betrayal. He was a trusted high-ranking officer who, during the American Revolution, switched sides and fought with the British against the soldiers he once commanded.

In addition, right here in Jamaica, there is still a raging debate about whether or not the Maroons, who had signed a "peace" treaty with the British in 1739 to return runaway slaves, were traitors. The jury is still deliberating.

But, as seen in the biblical story of ***Jesus Arrested***, Judas must be the number one traitor of all times. He is known all over the world and across several generations for betraying Jesus Christ. Just imagine if you had a good friend, a BFF even, part of your inner circle, and they sold you out for their own selfish agenda. And for what? Thirty pieces of silver.

Moreover, to add insult to injury, Judas not only betrays Jesus, but the sign of his betrayal was a kiss. Matthew 26:48-49 says, *"Now he who was betraying Him gave them a sign, saying, 'whomever I shall kiss, He is the man; seize Him.' And immediately he went to Jesus and said, 'Hail, Rabbi!' and kissed Him."*

A kiss is usually a symbol of love and affection reserved for family and friends. Thanks to Judas, it is also the origin of the well-known phrase, the "kiss of death," which in recent past was popularized by the Italian mob.

The biblical account of the betrayal of Judas also appears in Mark 14:43-50 and Luke 22:47-53. It marks a critical turning point as was prophesied by even Christ Himself.

There are many lessons in this passage. Nevertheless, I want to focus on one of the positive takeaways for me, that is, we should have compassion for our enemies, in spite of, just as Jesus did. You see, Jesus knew that Judas would betray Him, yet He did not condemn him. Jesus even asked him why he was betraying Him. Jesus went even further by reattaching the ear of the soldier that impetuous Peter chopped off, even though he was part of the mob who came to arrest Jesus following the betrayal. That is love.

Moreover, friend, do not think too harshly of Judas. We too betray Jesus in our time and in our lives repeatedly. When we fail to love one another, we betray Him. When we lie, cheat or steal, we betray Him. When we malice our brother, sister or friend, we betray Him. When we gossip or circulate hurtful information on social media, we betray Him. When we badmouth our co-workers, we betray Him. When we do not give food, drink, or shelter to others, even though we can, we betray Him.

Thank God Jesus knows our traitorous heart, yet still He loves us and yearns for us to come to Him. Even Judas showed remorse. Recognizing the burden and finality of his error, he took his own life. That was clearly the wrong way of dealing with the error of his way. What we should do whenever we betray Christ is to ask for His forgiveness and follow Him. He is willing and waiting to forgive us and to be compassionate towards us, just as He was willing to forgive Judas and was compassionate towards the soldier who lost his ear.

So, friend, there is really only one model to follow to guide us on the right path, away from betrayal and towards loyalty and faithfulness, and that is the Lord Jesus Christ. Not me, not our religious leaders, and certainly not our political leaders. Christ alone. He is the way, the truth, and the life. He gives us the kiss of life.

Reflection of Matthew 20:29-34

He Makes the Blind See

"There is so much trouble in the world..." These are words of Bob Marley, which were echoed by Prime Minister, Mia Motley, of Barbados at the 2022 Summit of the Americas. Sadly, friend, today, those words still ring true. So many crises are blinding the world. Right now, we are dealing with the global big three of COVID-19, Climate Change, and Crime, plus wars in Ukraine and the Middle East that are affecting the entire world. Jamaica is no exception. There was a news story in 2023 of the savage murder of a family of five, including four innocent children. It sent shockwaves throughout the entire nation. The world seems to be blinded by so much hate, envy, and greed.

The passage in Matthew 20:29-34 tells the story of ***Two Blind Men Receiving Sight*** by Jesus. Similar stories appear in Mark 10:46-52 and Luke 18:35-43 with minor variations. The other two Gospels speak of one blind beggar receiving sight. However, as we say in Jamaica, "If it nuh goh so, it nearly goh so." Therefore, whether it was one blind beggar or two does not really matter. What is important for me is that even the blind could see that Jesus is the Lord and Saviour. Moreover, they just had to cry out to Him, *"Lord, Son of David, have mercy on us!"*

Meris Haughton

What about us as we face all these crises? We too should be crying out to Jesus today, just as the two blind men in biblical times did.

It is not just about physical blindness. You see, so many other things also blind or burden us. Many of us have lost loved ones, are struggling financially, are lonely, are going through sickness, have lost our sense of direction or just dealing with the constant troubles of the world. There are some who are blinded by power, politics, self-importance, or by riches, sometimes even by life itself. The important thing is for us to recognise that we need help. As the saying goes, "Knowing is half the battle." The other half is to know that there is a risen Christ who can help us. Additionally, just as Jesus asked them then, He is asking us too, *"What do you want me to do for you?"*

"Lord," they answered, *"we want our sight."* We too should recognise that there is a better way. We also want to be able to see the beauty and wonder of nature, to experience the kindness of others, to watch our children grow to become accomplished adults, to love one another, and to live.

The scripture says, *"Jesus had compassion on them and touched their eyes. Immediately they received their sight and followed him." (Matthew 20:34).*

Yes, friend. Our Lord is compassionate. He hears our cries. So, let us take our blindness to Him. As the song by Andrae

From the Pews

Crouch says, *"Jesus is the answer for the world today. Above Him there's no other, Jesus is the way."*

If you have questions, call on Him. If you are discouraged, call on Him. If you cannot find peace, call on Him. If you are suffering pain or grief, call on Him. If you are in a dark place, call on Him. If you are troubled, call on Him. Just say, "Lord, have mercy on me, on us." He will touch our eyes, lips, hearts, and even our souls.

So, let us pray that our nation and us are healed of our different kinds of blindness. Oh, Lord, have mercy on us and help us to see the light, as without vision, the people perish.

Jesus is the way, the truth, and the life. CALL ON HIM.

Reflection of John 9:18-41

Lord, Heal Our Spiritual Blindness

The Bible has many references to Jesus healing the blind, but this particular passage has a deeper meaning as it also addresses the subject of *spiritual blindness*.

What is spiritual blindness? Spiritual blindness is a condition that an individual has when they are unable to see God or understand His message.[1] Although God is working all around us and showing us His glory, some people cannot perceive His divine work. In short, those who reject Christ are spiritually blind and are lost.

As you can imagine, spiritual blindness leads to all manner of ills. We saw this repeatedly with the Pharisees. For example, in John 9:34, they tossed a man out of the Synagogue because they refused to believe that Jesus had healed him of his physical blindness. They were obviously the blind ones, as they could not see the Son of Man who was right in front of them.

Nevertheless, spiritual blindness is not confined to the pages and the times of the Bible. Alas, with all the manners of evil happening in Jamaica today, you have to wonder if the whole country is blind. You just have to turn on the news on

---

[1] compellingtruth.org

any given day, and there are stories of murder, poverty, gang war, corruption, domestic violence; you name it. Damion Junior Gong Marley, in his reggae song "Welcome to Jamrock" sings of some harsh truths of our island paradise. In one stanza, it says, "Welcome to Jam down. Poor people ah dead at random. Political violence caan done. Pure ghost and phantom. The youth dem get blind by stardom." I like the positivity of the following line, "Now the Kings of kings ah call."

Jesus, the King of kings, is calling. He is calling us to repentance, just as John the Baptist did in the wilderness. He is waiting for us to see Him and to have a relationship with Him. Yes, Jesus wants us to see the light.

How great it is when we can see past all the darkness and see the light. It brings to mind the encouraging words of the song, "*I can see clearly now the rain is gone*" by the famed Country Singer, Johnny Nash, and covered by several artists. Call me biased, my favourite is the version by Jamaican Jimmy Cliff done for the movie *Cool Runnings*; a movie about the first Jamaican Bobsled team. It is a song about hope and courage for people who have experienced adversity in their lives but have later overcome it.

Yes, friend, like the song says, "I can see clearly now the rain is gone. I can see all obstacles in my way. Gone are the dark clouds that had me blind. It's gonna be a bright, bright, bright sun-shiny day." Thank God for His mercies.

You see, often it is when we are not able to see physically or figuratively that we must call upon the Lord to guide us out of our darkness into His marvellous light. We literally have to, as Apostle Paul said in 2 Corinthians 5:7, *"Walk by faith, not by sight." (KJV)*.

I imagine Paul knows this from personal experience. When he was Saul and zealously persecuting the Christians, the light of Christ on the road to Damascus struck him down. In that encounter, he became physically blind. That was when he gained spiritual sight. For the first time he was able to see clearly as his dark clouds were gone.

What of us, my friend? What of us? We have to ask God to open our eyes and hearts so we can see the truth and goodness of God that is all around us. What a glorious exclamation it would be if we could also say, *"I was blind but now I see."*

Reflection of Matthew 14:22-36

Keep Our Eyes on Jesus

The passage known as *Jesus Walks on Water* is in the Good Book. The Bible is indeed a good book. It is an amazing collection of sixty-six books, with very different styles. It contains the messages God desires us to have.

It is a good book because it is exciting to read. It captures historical events, stretches the imagination, and has many stories of ordinary people doing extraordinary things. It gives an account of everyday situations of the good, the bad, and the ugly. Most importantly, it shares the good news of Jesus Christ and teaches many lessons. What more could you want in a book?

According to the Guinness Book of World Records, as of 1995, the Bible is the bestselling book of all time with an estimated five billion copies sold and distributed worldwide and in many different languages.

The account of *Jesus Walks on the Water* must have resonated with the disciples. It appears in three of the four gospels (Matthew, Mark, and John). The version from Matthew is a wonderful story of prayer, fear, doubt, miracle, love, understanding, trust, faith, worship, and healing. I will focus on just a few verses.

Matthew 14:24 tells us that the boat the disciples were in *"was already a considerable distance from land, buffeted by the waves because the wind was against it."* In other words, the sea was rough because the weather was stormy.

So, think of poor Peter. Put yourself in his place and imagine being in a boat in the middle of the sea surrounded by water. It was dark with high winds rocking the boat. If that was not scary enough, out of nowhere, there appeared someone walking on the water towards you. I don't know about you, but, like Peter, I would probably think it was a ghost. The lyrics of Ernie Smith's song, *"It must be a duppy or a gunman. I never stop to see. Quarrie was a bwoy to I man, him couldn't follow me"* comes to mind. Of course, the disciples in the boat had nowhere to run, even though they were obviously full of fear.

Think about it. We all experience our own storms that rock our boats, causing fear and uncertainty. The loss of a loved one, being out of a job, sickness, loneliness, the upsurge in violence, the discrimination, injustices and protests we see happening in the United States, and many other situations are frightening. However, Jesus is always nearby. He responded to Peter, as He does to us daily, *"Take courage! It is I. Do not be afraid." (see Matthew 14:27).*

I know that it is sometimes hard to believe even the miracles that are before our eyes. We tell ourselves that it is too good to be true. We have doubts and want further proof.

From the Pews

In Matthew 14:28, Peter says, *"Lord, if it is you, tell me to come to you on the water."* Jesus answers and says, *"Come,"* and Peter obeys. That is faith.

Like Peter, we often turn our eyes on Jesus and obey Him only for a while. Then when things start going our way, we often turn away. Our own proverbial winds of life distract us. Work, family, fun, fortune, sometimes even church consumes us, and we lose sight of God. That is when we begin to sink into stress, distress, worry, anxiety, and other negative behaviours, sometimes even feeling like we are drowning.

No matter what we are going through, we only need to say like Peter, *"Lord save me!"* (see Matthew 14:30). Jesus will reach out His hand and rescue us. Even though the Lord may question how little faith we have sometimes, just like He did Peter, He, more than anyone, understands that to err is human and to forgive is divine.

We will have our doubts. We will face our storms. But Jesus is able to save us, not once, not twice, but as many times as we ask.

So, have faith. Keep your eyes on Jesus, and you will be able to face your storms without fear. I remember seeing written somewhere, "It is better to worship than worry." That is exactly what Philippians 4:6 means when it says, *"Do not be anxious about anything, but in every situation, by prayer*

Meris Haughton

and petition, with thanksgiving, present your requests to God."

As long as we depend on God and His power, we will be able to walk on the water and calm our storms.

CHAPTER 5

OBSERVANCES OF LIFE

"Ye observe days, and months, and times, and years."
(Galatians 4:10 – KJV).

As a people, we should always remember to observe important days in our nation and to honour all those on whose shoulders we stand.

Thank You, Lord, for our forefathers and mothers who paved the way for us all and those who continue to support us.

Reflection of Matthew 22:15-22

Work and Pay

Labour Day is an annual holiday to celebrate the achievements of workers. Labour Day has its origins in the labour union movement, specifically the eight-hour day movement, which advocated eight hours for work, eight hours for recreation, and eight hours for rest.

In an article published in The National Library of Jamaica, it states that, "Since 1890, May 1 has been reserved by many countries as the day to officially honour the Labour movement." Some countries chose different days in May or, like the United States and Canada, in September to celebrate it. In Jamaica, Labour Day is on May 23 each year. Over the years, it is observed in different ways. Previously, it was a public holiday where people rested from work, stayed home, or went on excursions. However, in recent times, it is an occasion to labour for others by doing community service.

The passage of **Paying Taxes to Caesar** is Jesus' response to one of the many trick questions He was asked. The debate of whether paying taxes to a government is righteous rages on today just as it did in biblical times. As a key spokesperson for Jamaica's Tax Authority, I could tell you all the benefits of paying taxes, but that would take time. As a practicing Christian, I will say that we are all called to pay our fair share for the collective good of all. We have to work and pay. Besides, if I could borrow a phrase from a recent episode of the Anglican Diocesan programme *Think on These Things*, "We should respect state authority, whilst we obey the commandments of God."

As a case in point, there is an inspiring movie that I have watched several times, which is a good example of this. The movie *Hacksaw Ridge* is a 2016 war drama that shares the true story of Private First-Class Desmond T. Doss, who won the U.S. Congressional Medal of Honour, despite refusing to bear arms for religious reasons during WWII. Doss was drafted into the army but was ostracized and ridiculed by fellow soldiers for his pacifist stance in refusing to carry a gun. Nevertheless, he went on to earn respect and adoration for his bravery, selflessness, and compassion after he risked his own life—without firing a shot—to save seventy-five men in the Battle of Okinawa. Wow! Although war is hell, it is a powerful story that demonstrates that we can live in this world without compromising our Christian values and principles.

This is what I believe Jesus was trying to teach His interrogators then and is teaching us still. We must recognise that we live in this world, and as such, we should obey the laws of the land. So, yes, we pay taxes to the authorities, just as we pay tithes, offerings, mission share—or any other name that is used—to the church. Because, just as taxes allows a government to provide goods and services for its people, tithes allow a church to provide outreach programmes for the community it serves and to run and maintain the church. So, the statement made popular on a political campaign trail some years ago that, "It takes cash to care" is as true for a government as it is for the church.

There is a big difference though. Taxes are a legal obligation, while tithes are a moral obligation. I learnt recently that the word *tithe* literally means tenth in Hebrew. Leviticus 27:30 says, "*A tithe of everything from the land, whether grain from the soil or fruit from the trees, belongs to the Lord; it is holy to the Lord.*" We are therefore morally obligated to give 10% of what we earn, grow, or have.

Jesus is asking us to give more than our treasure when He asks us to give to God what is God's. He is also asking us to give of our time and talents. So, if you can sing, sing to the Lord. If you can cook or bake, fix food for a soup kitchen. If you can preach, share the Word of God. If you like to serve, volunteer to work in a church group or programme. Do something; give something. Christ is asking us to give our very life to Him.

Moreover, friend, never forget that we who are blessed should be a blessing to others. We should therefore give generously and give from our hearts. As 2 Corinthians 9:7 says, "*Each of you should give what you have decided in your heart to give, not reluctantly or under compulsion, for God loves a cheerful giver.*" *(NIV)*.

So, as workers, whenever we observe Labour Day, let us remember that the Bible says in Acts 20:35, "*In all things I *have shown you that by working hard in this way we must help the weak and remember the words of the Lord Jesus, how he himself said, 'It is more blessed to give than to receive.'" (ESV).*

Reflection of Mark 7:24-37

Emancipendence of a Nation

Jamaica observes Emancipation from slavery on August 1, and celebrates our Independence on August 6. Locals refer to the period of August 1–6 as our Emancipendence. In homage to the Emancipendence season, during this period, persons sometimes read from the Jamaican Bible using the poetry of the Jamaican Patois. However, no matter the translation used, there is one common message in the two stories, **The Faith of a Syrophoenician Woman** and **The Healing of a Deaf and Mute Man**, that clearly shows that Jesus is the Great Physician. He is able to heal by speaking it into being from afar, as He did for the demon-possessed girl because of the faith of her mother. He is also able to heal by the laying of hands on someone, if we ask on their behalf. Jesus did it for the deaf-mute, based on his friends begging Him to intervene.

Friend, this cry for Jesus' healing mercy is so needed in our nation today. At every turn, you hear of someone else who is facing a health challenge, whether it is cancer, COVID-19 or something else. In one week, a ninety-plus-year-old cousin shared with me that she was recently diagnosed with cancer. Then, a few days later, my favourite aunt dislocated her hip just from turning badly.

From the Pews

I am sharing these two stories as, in both cases, persons interceded to God to heal them. In the first case, my elder cousin is no longer anxious and is in good spirits. In the second case, Jesus, through the healing hands of the ER doctors, laid hands on my aunt and put her hip back into position.

As we celebrate Emancipendence, I want to talk of healing of another kind; the healing of our nation. Sadly, we see that in spite of Emancipation in 1838, many in our land are still mentally shackled. This is contributing to too many persons blaming others for their not progressing in life. As our National Hero, Marcus Mosiah Garvey, said—which was later popularized in a song by the great reggae icon, Bob Marley—we have to "Emancipate ourself from mental slavery. None but ourselves can free our mind." That is right, "We should have no fear for atomic energy," and might I add war, crime, climate change, pandemic, or anything else of this world, "because none of them can stop the time."

That is right, friend; only God knows when the world, as we know it, will end. In the meantime, Jesus can heal our world and our minds if we only believe.

Whenever we celebrate Jamaica's Independence, let us beg Jesus to heal our nation from being deaf to the cries of our children who are hurting and dying, and from being deaf to the call from civil society for citizens to display greater values and attitudes. Let us cry to Jesus to heal us from being mute, to loosen our tongues to cry out against injustices meted out to the poor and marginalized, and to speak up against the vulgar comments and crass behaviour of some of our public officials.

As former Jamaican Prime Minister, PJ Patterson, issued in a rare statement, "We need to live up to our prayerful National Anthem and ask God to 'teach us true respect for all.'"

Yes, together, through the grace of God, we can heal Jamaica, land we love, and make it a better place. As our Governor General, Sir Patrick Allen, once said in an Independence Day message, "There is nothing wrong with Jamaica that cannot be fixed by what is right with Jamaica." Friend, he is so right. Jamaica has a lot to celebrate.

I feel proud and blessed that our small island nation is doing big things on the world stage. Just look at the consistency of our Sunshine Girls in World Netball and our Reggae Girls in the 2023 Women's World Cup Football, and we always look forward to the performance of our athletes at the World Championships and the Olympics. These positive displays of the black, green, and gold continue to be that medicine of hope for us.

I encourage you to remain hopeful. Whatever sickness we are experiencing personally and in our land, Jesus, the real good doctor, is on the job. I pray that through the grace of the Great Physician, our nation is healed individually and collectively. Yes, Jesus is the answer for the world today, just as He was yesterday and will be tomorrow. HE HEALS.

Reflection of Luke 10:25-37

Not All Heroes Wear a Cape

Jamaica's National Heroes' Day, observed annually in October, always make me think of the age-old question, "Who is my neighbour?" The answer is rooted in scripture. In fact, the second greatest commandment, next to loving God with all our heart, mind, strength, and soul, is to love our neighbour as our self (see Luke 10:27). This was and still is the premise on which Christianity stands.

Yes, friend, in Luke 10:27, Jesus, in answering the question, "What must I do to inherit eternal life?" says, *'Love the Lord your God with all your heart and with all your soul and with all your strength and with all your mind'*; and *'Love your neighbour as yourself.'*

Who is our neighbour?

The parable known as **The Good Samaritan** is one of the most well-known parables in the Bible. Jesus uses it as a teaching moment to show that people, then and now, should love everyone, including the rich man, poor man, beggar man, thief, and everyone in between.

Nevertheless, knowing it and living it are two very different things. Truthfully, some people are hard to love, really hard. I struggle with loving some persons who rub me the wrong way, like some of those aggressive window washers at the traffic light, those crazy taxi drivers on our roads, those pushy vendors, those annoying persons, and others we often have little regard for.

Hebrews 13:2 tells us, '*Do not forget to show hospitality to strangers, for by so doing some people have shown hospitality to angels without knowing it.*' As my cousin, Elder Richard, says, "Suppose they were placed at points in our lives to watch over us, to keep us from harm, to guard our souls? We could be chasing away God's angels."

You see, we should not reserve our love only for our friends and family. That is the easy part, well, most times. We need to be intentional about our kindness. Share it, even if there is no hope of getting it back in return. You would be surprised that often, it is the little things that count. We could start by being courteous and just acknowledging everyone we meet, no matter who or what they are.

We should also commit ourselves to looking around and noticing how we might be able to help someone out. We need to be like Christ, who often reached out to help and love the vulnerable; the blind, deaf, sick, even the woman at the well. We also need to have compassion and show kindness to strangers. This is what will really make a difference in the world.

Yes, there are still good Samaritans and modern-day heroes among us. During Jamaica's annual National Heroes' Day

Awards Ceremony, it always warms my heart to see the persons who receive the badge of honour for gallantry. One such story of courage and selflessness that really touched me was of Jeffery Bowen, who noticed a young boy trying to stay afloat in crocodile-infested waters in Bridgeport, St. Catherine. After several failed attempts to call out to the boy, Mr. Bowen jumped into the water, risking his own life to save the boy. He later discovered that the boy was hearing impaired. That was truly a Good Samaritan moment of divine intervention by a man now known as the 'Portmore Hero.' Truthfully, if you think about it, there are many unsung heroes, some we know personally. God knows our hearts.

Let me share a few simple heroic suggestions you could consider:

1. Donate blood as there is a chronic shortage of blood in our hospitals. As the saying goes, the next life you save may be your own.
2. Donate non-perishable food items and hygiene products for the needy. We have a donation bin right by the front door of our church. Once a month we distribute food packages and, friend, the demands are ever growing.
3. Call or visit an elderly neighbour or church member. Loneliness is one of their biggest challenges, so reach out and touch someone.
4. Volunteer at your alma mater or in a school near you. Our nation's schools need our support.

5. Mentor a child, as many of our children need some proper guidance. You just have to turn on the news to see the crises facing our children.

There are so many other ways that we can be neighbours and everyday heroes. So, be a hero, be a friend, be a neighbour. Build acts of kindness into your busy schedule. This can change not just the life of others, but it can change your life too.

Never forget that as dark as our world seems sometimes, there is still a lot of light shining through. So, let your light SHINE before others so they may see your good work.

Reflection of John 3:1-21

Old Time Christmas

"For God so loved the world that he gave his one and only Son, that whoever believes in him shall not perish but have eternal life." (John 3:16).

This is probably one of the most quoted verses from the Bible. People sometimes just simply say "John 3:16" without even saying the actual verse, as it is so well known. But how many persons stop to think that it tells of a perfect gift of love? This is exactly what Jesus shared with Nicodemus in the story **Jesus Teaches Nicodemus**.

John 3:16 is a verse that shows how deep God's love for us is—a deep sacrificial love for people, who mostly did not even care about Him. That is who God is.

During the season of Christmas, it is the perfect time to reflect on this wonderful gift. God loved the world so much, flaws and all, that He gave us His one and only or, as we say in Jamaica, "one deggae-deggae" Son, in exchange for the salvation of all people, for all time. We should do as Psalm 136:1 tells us and, *"Give thanks to the Lord, for he is good. His love endures forever."* This gives us faith in a gift that keeps on giving, that extends to you and me.

God's love is not a free pass for us to do as we like. If we do falter—and being human, we will—rest assured that we can ask for forgiveness, as God's love remains steadfast.

God's gift of love, grace, and undeserved mercy is a fitting example for all of us. As disciples of Christ, we should be rooted and grounded in love; a love that we should pay forward by showing love to others. What better time to show love than the Christmas season?

Christmas actually holds an extra special meaning for me. In addition to God's gift of His Son, I am also thankful for God's gift of my mom, who was also born on Christmas Day. That is an extra reason I love the season.

Mom shared with me her love for Christmas, especially those wonderful Jamaican traditions of Christmas carols, decorations, cakes, sorrel, ham, gungo rice and peas, and wearing the colour red, which I tend to do all month. I just love it all. She also passed on the love of God and the spirit of family togetherness, and showing extra love for others at Christmas. It is probably why one of my favourite Christmas Songs is "Give Love on Christmas Day." So, when people see me in a Santa hat and ask what I am giving them for Christmas, without hesitation, I can honestly tell them LOVE.

Even though I cannot sing very well, I like to sing that part in the song which says, "What the world needs is love. Yes, the world needs your love…No greater gift is there than love." This is so true. We have so many opportunities to show love.

I remember one Sunday morning during Christmas, a church brother asked if I could arrange to get some clothes, bed linen, and towels for someone in need. These are things we take for granted, but they mean the world to others.

During the COVID-19 crazy Christmases, the needs heightened. There are many ways, as individuals and as a community, that we can give love to our neighbours. We can donate clothes or toys to a child whose parents cannot afford to buy them. Give groceries to a family that is struggling financially. Provide a meal for a homeless person who has no family. Phone a friend who is sick or a shut-in. Contact a church brother or sister who could do with some good cheer. Even just smile and nod hello to a stranger to show we care.

Yes, 'tis the season of giving, but let us remember too that giving love isn't reserved for just Christmas Day. Love is a gift that we should keep on giving every minute of every hour of every day.

So as CHRISTians, let us give love, not just at CHRISTmas. Let us take time to show the love of God to someone today and every day. I am not asking us to save the world. But if each one helps one, imagine how much better the world could be, giving us HOPE for humanity.

The next time someone says John 3:16, just remember it is a message of Faith, Hope, and Love, but the greatest of these is LOVE (see 1 Corinthians 13:13).

CHAPTER 6

PRINCIPLES OF LIFE

"So now faith, hope, and love abide, these three; but the greatest of these is love." (1 Corinthians 13:13).

There are several principles of good Christian living that we can find in the Bible to guide us and help us to grow our personal relationship with God.

The biblical blueprint will also help us to live right with others as we navigate our life.

Reflection of Mark 11:12-25

Faith and Forgiveness

The scripture passage entitled *Jesus Curses a Fig Tree and Clears the Temple Courts* is rich with many life lessons. For this brief reflection, I am going to focus on the "F-words"; Faith and Forgiveness.

Before we get to a place of faith and forgiveness, let me just say that I have always appreciated the humanness of Christ. We saw Him being hungry, annoyed, and vexed to the point of overturning the tables of the money changers and driving out the vendors who upset Him by turning the church into a "den of thieves." These are all feelings and emotions that we can identify with.

As we turn our attention to faith, I must admit that *"Have Faith in God" (see Mark 11:22)* is actually one of my mantras that is shared by others.

My family, especially my niece, Gabrielle, who lost her adopted mom at the age fifteen, has been, and is going through a lot. Nevertheless, as I often remind her, every problem has a solution. Just pray and have faith. Thanks be to God, through it all, she has not lost her faith.

In preparing this meditation, I asked Gabrielle what she understands when Jesus says to His disciples *"Have faith in*

God." She shared with me that, for her, "It's important to have faith in God no matter what." She continued to say, "It's not like trusting people who sometimes let you down, but when you have faith in God, all things are possible." That is wisdom from the mouth of babes. Mind you, she is not exactly a babe as we had this conversation on the day she turned sixteen. It was actually her idea that her special day included worship. Therefore, weeks before her natal day, she asked me to lead evening prayer and share a special meditation as part of her celebration. You see, she is aware that I do this to mark other special days.

Unfortunately, our church administrator brought to my attention that our Brotherhood of St. Andrew (BSA) men's group was already rostered to lead that day. I prayed about how to resolve the situation, as I didn't want to disappoint my niece. But, on hearing of the dilemma, the BSA was gracious and understanding in allowing me to lead on what was their scheduled time on the roster. My prayer was answered. That, too, is a show of faith. As it is written, *"Therefore I tell you, whatever you ask for in prayer, believe that you have received it, and it will be yours." (Mark 11:24).* This is something Christ is telling all of us.

It is a given that we will go through challenges and, sometimes, we will get knocked down in life, but there is always a way to get back up. We just need to *"Have faith in God."* Yes, God is good all the time; all the time, God is good.

The basic meaning of faith is trust and commitment in God. It is taking God at His Word. Hebrews 11 is known as the FAITH chapter.

A Google search revealed that—depending on the version of the Bible—the word FAITH appears over two hundred and fifty times. This is not counting the derivatives, like *faithful* or *faithfully*. Other similar words like *believe* were not factored in either. Any way you spin it, faith appears a lot of times.

There have been many people of faith throughout biblical times. Abraham demonstrated his faith when God told him to sacrifice his son. He knew God would supply a lamb. Noah showed faith in building an Ark when there was no rain in the forecast. David showed faith that he could slay a giant with a slingshot. What about you, my friend? We too can demonstrate faith in our everyday life.

In showing faith, Christ also asks us to forgive others. Yes, friend, faith and forgiveness go hand in hand. Just as God forgives us, we should forgive others. Mark 11:25 says, *"And when you stand praying, if you hold anything against anyone, forgive them, so that your Father in heaven may forgive you your sins."* This sentiment is echoed in our church's greeting of the peace, "If you are offering your gift at the altar, and there remember that your brother has something against you, leave your gift there before the altar and go; first be reconciled to your brother, and then come and offer your gift." In other words, it is not right to keep malice. Be at peace, for your own sake, as well as for others.

Forgiveness is not a one-off command. In Matthew 18:21-22, Jesus actually told the disciples that we should forgive our brothers seventy times seven. Personally, I do not believe He literally meant 490 times, but we should forgive again and again.

Therefore, friend, have faith and forgive to live in and through Christ.

Reflection of Matthew 12:14-21

Hope and Expectation

During what is observed as the Feast of Epiphany, I am reminded of the three wise men following the star to pay homage to baby Jesus, born to save us all. They had their epiphany then, which is described as a time when something is shown, displayed or manifested to others. What of us in our time? What of our epiphany? By journeying through the Bible and through life, we can have our own epiphany of the hope of salvation in Christ. We just need to open our eyes and hearts, then share with others.

Matthew 12:14-21, in some translations, is entitled **God's Chosen Servant**. It clearly shows us that, *"In his name the nations will put their hope." (see Matthew 12:21)*. There are many other biblical references to hope in the Bible. One of my all-time favourites is Romans 15:13, *"May the God of hope fill you with all joy and peace as you trust in Him, so that you may overflow with hope by the power of the Holy Spirit."* Another is Hebrews 11:1, *"Now faith is being sure of what we hope for and certain of what we do not see."* There is also Psalms 71:14 that says, *"As for me, I will always have hope; I will praise you more and more."*

As we journey through life, never forget the four powerful resources we have within us: Love, Prayer, a Positive

Attitude and, of course, **Hope**. That is right, friend, we should always live in hope.

Interestingly, someone in my community group shared a message of hope as I reflected on this passage. It reminded me that believers are born into a living hope. So, in spite of the trials and tribulations we face individually, as a community, a church, a nation, and even globally, in Christ, we have the foundation for our expectations and desires to be realised. It may not be today, tomorrow, this year, or the next, but through Christ, ALL things are possible.

As believers, we must anchor our hope in the solid rock of Jesus Christ. His Word is always true, and His promises are always kept. So let us not focus on the negatives of crime, accidents, cancers, and other maladies plaguing our nation today, but instead focus on Jesus, who is a God of hope. He answers prayers. As Christians, when we make a request and submit to God, we will always get an answer: yes, no or wait.

Life can be hard. We sometimes ask the question, "Why?" But the Lord does not disappoint those who seek His will. There are good things in store for us. Jeremiah 29:11 says, *"For I know the plans I have for you"*, declares the Lord, *"plans to prosper you and not to harm you, plans to give you hope and a future."* Friend, we cannot even hope for ourselves as much good as God has in store. Look how God prospered Job, who was sorely tested; he never lost hope.

Meris Haughton

The best choice a Christian can make is to fix his or her hope in the Lord Jesus Christ.

Always remember that when one door closes, another will open with something better for us. So, welcome whatever fits His will for your life and turn away from all that does not. Yes, circumstances may shift and change, but Jesus never changes. He is a living hope who never disappoints.

As we live our lives, consider these recommendations found in Romans 12:12 and put them at the top of your list, *"Be joyful in hope, patient in affliction, faithful in prayer."*

A Prayer of HOPE for Today

Father, thank You that our eternal future is built upon Christ Jesus, our Lord. Thank You that we can hold on to the hope that we have in Him. May we never forget on whom our hope is founded, knowing that He died for our sins so that we may live.

Lord, in Your mercy. **Hear our Prayer.**

May we stand firm on the confession of our faith and develop a living hope that stands fast in the day of trouble, knowing that in Him, we can face all that this life throws at us.

Lord, in Your mercy. **Hear our Prayer.**

Lord, help us to keep the light of Jesus in our hearts so that we may not lose hope. The world may not see this hope right now, but through us, may they discover and know the eternal hope of our Lord and Saviour.

Lord, in Your mercy. **Hear our Prayer.**

Reflection of Luke 10:25-37

Love Thy Neighbour

"*Love your neighbour as yourself*" is the central theme of the well-known parable of *The Good Samaritan*.

People love to say that charity begins at home, or in the Jamaican parlance, "Parson christen him pickney fuss." However, we are also called to do good for everyone, not just our family and friends.

In the context of the biblical story, we see the Samaritan rescuing not just any stranger but a man considered his enemy based on where he was from. Hence the term "the Good Samaritan." Today, the phrase is synonymous with someone doing good deeds or charitable works for someone they may not know, simply out of their love for humanity and being a neighbour.

Throughout my life, living close to good neighbours is a blessing. Some have become more like family, for example, my childhood neighbour, Layton, who is my brother from another mother. I am also thankful for my neighbours in adulthood, like "Aunty Pearline" in my community and a host of others. As neighbours, we look out for each other. One of my blood aunts, who spent a couple of months with me, even commented on how neighbourly my community is.

Nevertheless, it is easy to be kind and do good deeds for our family and friends and for others we know, but what of persons we are not friends with or those we don't even know? Should we not be neighbourly with them too? Yes, we should. That was the point of the parable shared by Jesus.

Truthfully, it is not always easy. Some people just rub you the wrong way. I have been guilty on occasions for looking away when a beggar or windshield wiper approached me on the street or at a traffic light. That was not neighbourly at all. On the other hand, simply saying you will pray on hearing the news of someone who is suffering or in need but you fail to do so is also not neighbourly.

Prayer is good, but it is not always enough. The commandments in the Bible challenge us to look within and stretch ourselves to do more. None is more taxing as the commandment to love our neighbours as ourselves. Both the Old and the New Testaments refer to this. In fact, Mark 12:29-31 tells us that this is the second greatest commandment, after the commandment to love God.

It is the love of thy neighbour mentality that led four young men to risk their lives to save a twelve-year-old girl from being swept away by a flash flood during the 2021 rainy season in Jamaica. They sprang into action after soldiers stationed in the area reportedly said, "They were limited in resources to assist." Although the men were from the same community, they did not know the girl. But one of them said that when he saw her clutching onto a branch, he had to brave the floodwaters because he was a father, and it could have been his child. Their selfless act was a living example of loving thy neighbour and being a Good Samaritan.

We should be encouraged to do more. If we see someone in need, say something, do something.

This brings to mind a line in the Jamaica National Anthem that urges us to "Stand up for justice, brotherhood, and peace, and to play our part in advancing the welfare of the whole human race." These are qualities of a Good Samaritan.

I challenge you, just as I challenge myself, to intentionally be a Good Samaritan. Do selfless acts without expecting a reward or recognition (see Matthew 6:3). There are lots of opportunities, especially during these difficult times. It doesn't have to be something big. You could phone someone you haven't seen for a while as they could be experiencing loneliness, sponsor a care package for a mother struggling to feed her family because she lost her job, or share your Wi-Fi with a child next door who can't afford data to access school online. The point is, if we can do something good, as the Nike ad says, "JUST DO IT" today, tomorrow, and every day.

Put into practice the golden rule we learnt in Sunday school, "Do unto others as you'd have them do unto you." As my mother of blessed memory used to say, "There but for the grace of God go I."

We should share our love with neighbours. After all, we are each other's keeper.

Reflection of John 17:9-19

The Power of Prayer

"*Lord, I pray. I honour Your name. Deliver Your mercies. Whenever I fall, You pick me up. Glory to Thee, oh God.*" These are lines of that powerful Wayne Marshall reggae gospel song and, I could even say, my life's theme song.

Prayer should be the most important conversation of the day. We should take it to God before we take it to anyone else. Just to give you an idea of how important prayer was in biblical times, a quick Google search reveals that in the New King James Bible, the word "prayer" appears 87 times in 80 verses in the Old Testament. In the New Testament, it is mentioned 53 times in 53 verses. That is many times, not counting derivatives like *praying, prayed, prayers*; you get the picture.

It is my belief that the power of prayer is not in the prayer itself but in the grace of God. Moreover, we all need prayers, individually and collectively. In the story recorded in John 17:9 titled ***Jesus Prays for His Disciples***, Jesus said, "*I pray for them,*" as He does for all of us.

A deeper search revealed that Jesus prayed at least thirty-eight times in the Gospels. We have no greater example of the need for prayer than Jesus' example. We often see Jesus setting aside time to pray before and/or after a major event or performing a miracle or sign. He prayed for His friends and His enemies alike, as should we also.

In fact, even before being betrayed, Jesus prayed in the Garden of Gethsemane. Knowing what He was to face, He must have felt overwhelming sadness and anguish. In Matthew 26:39, He prayed, *"My Father, if it is possible, may this cup be taken from me. Yet not as I will, but as you will."* Luke 22:44 records, during His agony as he prayed, *"His sweat was like drops of blood falling to the ground."* Can you even imagine the depth of His anguish? Notwithstanding His pain, He also showed compassion in praying for forgiveness for His persecutors. As He was being crucified, in Luke 23:34, He prayed, *"Father, forgive them; for they know not what they are doing."* That is a lesson for all of us.

Praying is not difficult. It is really just a conversation with God. It is how we communicate our gratitude, hopes, dreams, fears, and burdens. But if you find it difficult to pray, do not be discouraged. Adding a tool or method to your prayer time can help to guide you and create a more intimate moment with God. I am not telling you how or when to pray, but pray we must.

Students of theology will tell you of different tools to pray. There is the S.O.A.P. method. That is using a journal to write out the **Scripture**, then **Observe** what it says, **Apply** it to your daily life, then write a **Prayer**. There is also the

A.C.T.S. method. That is a prayer of **Adoration, Confession, Thanksgiving, and Supplication**. Yet another simple tool is the five-finger prayer shared in my church's WhatsApp group recently. This guides you to pray for:

1. Family and friends
2. Teachers
3. Leaders
4. Those most in need
5. Yourself

I quite like this one as it covers all the bases. Additionally, our own Book of Common Prayer—a.k.a. the red book—used by the Anglican church in the Province of the West Indies (CPWI) has prayers for all seasons and reasons. That is why we use it as a guide for Evening Prayer and other liturgical services and rites. There are many others.

I remember one my surrogate grandfather of blessed memory used when he had gotten old and sick and no longer had the energy to put his thoughts together, much less to pray aloud. As his health declined, he had his caregiver paste some written prayers around his room, and he would simply point at one and say, *"This one today, Lord."* The Lord knows our hearts.

Friend, it really does not matter how we pray. I know sometimes we get intimidated when we hear some people beat their chest and pray some loud, long prayers. However, Jesus taught in Matthew 6:5-6, *"When you pray, do not be like the hypocrites, for they love to pray standing in the synagogues and on the street corners to be seen by men…but when you pray, go into your room, close the door and pray to your father who is unseen."*

Just find what, when, where, and how works for you. It doesn't have to be a special closet like in the movie *War Room*; it could be in your garden, it could be your bedroom, or even your bathroom. Just do you, and communicate with God in your own way.

If you are still unsure, do not let that deter you, as the Lord Himself taught us how to pray in Luke 11:2-4 in what is known as the Lord's Prayer. It is a perfect prayer.

So, friend, pray in your own way to build your relationship with God. In fact, your prayer can just be a conversation with God. In addition, remember, God hears our prayers. He may not answer in the way we want or when we want, but rest assured, He answers. He is with us always. He is with us through the hills and valleys of life.

Yes, we are called to live a life of dedicated prayer. Paul says, *"Pray continually; give thanks in all circumstances, for this is God's will for you in Christ Jesus." (1 Thessalonian 5:17-19).*

Therefore, I end as I started: "Lord, I pray. I honour Your name. Deliver Your mercies. Whenever I fall, You pick me up. Glory to Thee, oh God."

Reflection of Matthew 4:12-17

Repent and Be Friends with God Again

Since the dawn of time, the message of repentance has been told, and it has not changed. In the Old Testament, we had prophets like Isaiah proclaiming the word. In Isaiah 30:15, he says, *"In repentance and rest is your salvation, in quietness and trust is your strength..."* Throughout the New Testament, we see prophets like John the Baptist in Matthew 3:2 crying out in the wilderness, *"Repent, for the kingdom of heaven is near."* Even Jesus Himself proclaimed in Matthew 4:17, *"Repent, for the kingdom of heaven has come near." (NIV)*.

We too should be proclaiming the word of repentance. Moreover, in the season of Lent, we are invited to be rooted in and proclaiming the Word. There is no better time.

What does it really mean to repent? The Oxford dictionary says it means *to feel or express sincere regret or remorse about one's wrongdoing or sin.* From a biblical perspective, it means to rearrange your entire way of thinking, feeling, and being in order to forsake or give up what is wrong. I particularly like how the New Century Version translation of the Bible makes it abundantly clear. It says, *"Change your hearts and lives, because the kingdom of heaven is near." (Matthew 4:17)*. Moreover, pun intended, this is something we need to take to heart.

I read of a 4-step process to repentance, which makes perfect sense to me. It requires us to:

1. take responsibility for what we have done wrong.
2. regret and have remorse for our doing wrong.
3. resolve and be committed to not repeating the wrong.
4. repair the damage we have done wrong, apologising to the party we have wronged.

In addition, through repentance, we can build our relationship with God. In one of my recent morning devotions, one of the writers of *Our Daily Bread* told a story of how a mother explained to her young daughter that, "Repentance makes us friends with God again." I like that. It may sound simplistic, but is it not exactly what repentance is? The story goes on to say that at a special church service, the mother was embarrassed when her daughter clapped whenever anyone responded to the altar call to come up to ask for God's forgiveness. Is repentance not something to celebrate? Yes, it is. We should take our cue from that innocent child. In fact, Luke 15:10 says, *"There is rejoicing in the presence of the angels of God over one sinner who repents."*

There are other examples in the Good Book of the call for us to celebrate repentance. Think of the parable of the prodigal son. Jesus shared the story of the father who had a grand party—even killing the fattened calf—when the wayward son returned home. Friend, we too should clap, sing, and dance when someone gives their life to God or asks for forgiveness. As proclaimers, we need to help them and support each other on that journey.

We must remember that repentance is not a get-out-of-jail-free card—like in the game Monopoly—although we are saved by God's grace. Repentance is an honest, regretful acknowledgment of our sin with a commitment to change. Repentance leads us to develop godliness, while getting rid of habits that lead to sin. So, let us be true to ourselves and to God. Let us do it today, as tomorrow may be too late. Let us remember that Jesus said in Matthew 4:17, *"Repent, for the kingdom of heaven has come near."*

Reflection of Luke 16:10-16

Trust and Obey

In Jamaica, it is quite common to visit a corner or country shop and see a sign that reads, "God we trust. Everyone else pays cash." It may sound funny, but it is perfectly true. The ***Parable of The Shrewd Manager*** speaks of trust and honesty in people and that those who can be trusted or be honest with little can be trusted or be honest with a lot (see Luke 16:10-12). As wonderful as that is, that kind of trust and honesty in man and riches can easily be broken.

We must all strive to be trustworthy and honest. No one likes a dishonest person or someone you cannot trust. Personally, it is one of my pet peeves. But what does it really mean to trust? The Oxford dictionary defines trust as a firm belief in the reliability, truth, or ability of someone or something. That, my friend, is at the heart of faith: a belief and trust in God.

Nevertheless, I want to focus my attention on Luke 16:16, which reminds us that even in our time, we should be preaching the good news of the kingdom of God. This does not have to be from a pulpit or lectern. Also, it shouldn't be just what we say but how we live. As my pastor, Father Franklyn, often says, "Preach the Gospel always, sometimes using words."

Meris Haughton

If you think about it, we have so much to say in giving praise to our God. Recently, I saw someone I had not seen for a while, and she was radiating such joy. When I asked her how she was doing, she literally said, "God be praised, I'm well." She then spun around, touched her hair, and showed me what I thought was her hairstyle, which was a lovely short wash and wear cut. When I looked more closely, she had a scar. She then shared with me that the previous year, she had a brain aneurysm that almost took her life, but through the grace of God, the skill of her medical team, and the support of family and friends, she is here today to tell the tale. I told her that was such a powerful testimony, and she laughed and said she tells everybody she sees and encourages them to praise God.

We can all take a page out of her book, as I am sure we all have our own praise stories. I have so many. Every day I give God praise. Even in the midst of storms, just as He did for the disciples, He can say to the winds, "Be still," and they will obey. We can ALWAYS put our TRUST in GOD.

Undoubtedly, we face our own personal storms. We often face the threat of actual storms in Jamaica during the six-month hurricane season (June to November). We experience anxious moments whenever it rains heavily as flooding, loss of property, and loss of livelihood are possible. But, praise God, as my mom would say, "This too shall pass." We always hear and see those wonderful stories of compassion, neighbourliness, and love shown by others as they support others who, sometimes, they don't even know. Even in the midst of darkness, there is so much light. Do not take these things for granted. I urge you to share your stories to encourage others. As the song says, "**Every praise is to our God.**"

CHAPTER 7

MIRACLES OF LIFE

"But if I were you, I would appeal to God; I would lay my cause before him. He performs wonders that cannot be fathomed, miracles that cannot be counted." (Job 5:8-9).

Miracles happen every day. Life itself is a miracle. If we only open our eyes and minds, we will see that there are many miracles in our own lives.

Reflection on John 2:1-11

Jesus Changes Water to Wine

The passage of *Jesus Turns Water to Wine* is a favourite of many Jamaicans. Like the wedding at Cana, wine and other spirits are central to many celebratory occasions, such as our Independence, weddings, birthdays, and even when burying the dead.

The passage, found only in the Gospel of John, records Jesus' first miracle. It is actually one of the most well-known miracles in the Bible. It is such a well-known passage that even a drunk can quote from it.

Jesus uses the occasion of an ordinary wedding—which in biblical times, as it is today, is a happy ceremonial occasion that we can all identify with—to teach us extraordinary lessons of the Spirit of the living God and the gifts of belief, abundance, obedience, and faith.

The passage teaches us about belief.

The passage tells us, "W*hen the wine was gone,*" Jesus' mother told Him, "*They have no more wine.*" She was clearly not offended when He asked her, "*Dear woman, why do you involve Me?*" Knowing that He was the Son of God, she did not skip a beat when she told the servants, "*Do whatever He tells you.*" She did not know what He would do, but she obviously had the unfailing belief that He would make a way.

Have you ever been in a situation where you can see no way out? Where you did not know which way to turn? My grandmother, Muriel, used to say, "Put it in the hands of the Lord, and He will show you a way." Like Jesus' mother, we must have the belief that no matter what our circumstances, Jesus is a waymaker and a miracle worker. Moreover, miracles happen every day.

The passage also shows God's abundance.

There were six jars, which held about 150 gallons in total. Now, that was really a lot of wine. What it also shows is that God is able to supply all our needs and will bless us abundantly.

I remember when my father died, and we were planning for the repast. Now, my family is big and close-knit, plus my father knew many people, some who loved the spirits of the liquid kind. So, imagine planning how to cater for all these people without bankrupting the family. The Bible says, "*Ask and it will be given.*" (Matthew 7:7). One friend gave us two cases of assorted spirits, another gave us a goat, another gave a case of chicken, another gave about fifty pounds of fried fish, and yet another gave a big pot of soup. The Lord saw our need and blessed us abundantly.

The passage teaches us too about obedience.

Jesus tells the servants, *"Fill the jars with water,"* which they did. Then He instructed them to *"Draw some out and take it to the Master of the Banquet (MB),"* and they complied. It is when they heard the MB exclaim that the bridegroom had saved the best for last that they realized the miracle of the water turning to wine.

We need to be like the servants and trust and obey when the Lord speaks to us. Jesus speaks to us all the time. We just have to listen. We may not always understand the why, but in time, our own miracles will be revealed.

Finally, the passage speaks of faith.

After witnessing the miraculous sign, Jesus *"Revealed His glory, and His disciples put their faith in Him."* We too see signs of Jesus' glory every single day. Therefore, we too should have faith in our Lord and saviour.

I am sure we can all attest to personally seeing signs of Jesus' glory. It may not have been water turning to wine, but think about it. I know I have seen miraculous signs and wonders of Christ again and again. Like the disciples, we should also put our faith in Jesus.

I know we have moments when our faith falters, but hard times are often blessings in disguise. Look at what happened during the COVID-19 pandemic. We heard so many stories of estranged families becoming closer, distant neighbours now looking out for each other, busy people taking the time to check on the elderly and playing with their children, strangers reaching out and helping people they do not even know, corporate and government entities demonstrating greater corporate social responsibility, and many drawing closer to God. These are all miraculous signs of Jesus' glory. We just have to open our eyes to see when these happen. Keep the faith, my friend.

Reflection of Mark 6:30-46

Feed the People

The story of the *Feeding of the 5000* always reminds me of those big funerals or wedding gatherings I hear of in the country, where the whole community comes out, and they expect to get food to eat. I have seen this with my own eyes. I remember years ago when a grandaunt had died. In true Jamaican fashion, they had nine nights of gathering with people coming to her house and sharing stories, singing, playing dominoes and, of course, feeding the people. What was even more amazing to me was seeing some of the neighbours "tidying" their children and sending them across to my grandaunt's house for no other reason but to get dinner. I am sure this is the genesis of the Jamaican tradition of serving curry goat and rice. You see, you can always stretch the curry goat and put on another pot of rice to feed the proverbial 5000.

So, imagine really having 5000 people gathered in the middle of nowhere, and it is dinnertime, and there is only one small boy with his "shet pan" having anything to eat. Miraculously, this is how Jesus was able to feed the multitude of people. No wonder the feeding of the 5000 is also known as the miracle of the five loaves and two fish.

This phenomenon clearly resonated with the writers of the Gospel as the miracle is recorded in all four Gospels. It is in

Matthew 14:13–21, Mark 6:31–44, Luke 9:12–17 and John 6:1–14. Although there are minor differences in the details provided, what is common and unquestionable is that it is a miracle.

My friend, the miracle in Mark 6:30-46 was used to teach the thousands present in the wilderness, as it is teaching us too in our time, lessons of compassion, faith, and prayers.

In Mark 6:34, *"When Jesus landed and saw a large crowd, he had compassion on them, because they were like sheep without a shepherd. So, he began teaching them many things."* We should also have compassion on those around us who are in need. Moreover, friend, right now there are many opportunities as there is much need.

Mark 6:39 is a lesson in faith. It says, *"Then Jesus directed them to have all the people sit down in groups on the green grass."* They did not know what was going to happen, but they had the belief that something would. So, sit they did. We should have such faith in our time and in our lives. We may not be able to see what blessing is in store for us, but never forget that through Christ, all things are possible.

The Bible says faith and prayers can move mountains (see Matthew 17:20). Moreover, in Mark 6:41, we see that prayer can also make fish and bread multiply. It reads, *"Taking the five loaves and the two fish and looking up to heaven, he gave thanks and broke the loaves. Then he gave them to his disciples to distribute to the people. He also divided the two fish among them all."* My mom of blessed memory was a true believer in this principle. I was always amazed how many of our friends in the neighbourhood would eat from our pot, as they would coincidentally show up at mealtime, and mom would not turn anyone away. She would always say there is enough to share; just bless it and eat. She was never wrong. It always stretched, showing the power of prayer.

Yes, my friend, we have to take a slice of life from Christ and feed not just our physical hunger but also have some chicken soup for our soul and for others. In feeding ourselves, it allows us to be able to feed others. I use my Our Daily Bread devotional to feed my spirit in the mornings. It may not be a belly full, but it is a good way to break my nightly spiritual fast. This gives me the energy to worship, work, and witness.

My friend, remember the lessons in the story: have compassion for others, have faith in our God, and always give thanks and praise through prayer.

Reflection of Mark 9:2-13

Spiritual Change

The Merriam-Webster dictionary defines transfiguration as a *change in form or appearance: METAMORPHOSIS or an exalting, glorifying, or spiritual change.*

The account of the **Transfiguration of Jesus** not only appears in Mark 9:2-13, but it also appears in the other synoptic gospels (Matthew 17:1–8 and Luke 9:28–36). There is also a reference in 2 Peter 1:16–18. These multiple accounts represent the importance of the event.

The event is also referenced elsewhere in the New Testament that as believers, a similar sign can happen to us when we encounter God. Paul, the Apostle, in 2 Corinthians 3:18, speaks of the transformation of believers via *"beholding as in a mirror the glory of the Lord, are being transformed into the same image from glory to glory...." (NAS).* He should know as he had his own encounter when the dazzling light blinded him on the road to Damascus. This was when Saul, the Christian persecutor, was transformed to become Paul, the Christian proclaimer. He literally saw the light.

Even in the days of the Old Testament, we see believers by their encounter with God transforming. Exodus 34:29 says,

Meris Haughton

"When Moses came down from Mount Sinai with the two tablets of the covenant law in his hands, he was not aware that his face was radiant because he had spoken with the Lord."

In Jamaica, we celebrate February as Reggae Month, which reminds me that even in our time, there have been several stories of gospel artists who had a spiritual change to become and profess their Christianity through their music. Recording artiste, Lt. Stitchie, started singing gospel after almost dying in a car accident. Singer, Carlene Davis, had a spiritual calling. After his brother was murdered and his sister died in a car accident, Papa San turned to Christianity. In addition, there is the inspiring story of the artist, Prodigal Son. He was a former gangster who had a spiritual encounter and was inspired by the parable of the same name to fight for Christ.

We can have a spiritual experience in our life as well. That means we can encounter God, literally or figuratively, and have a spiritual change.

Peter, James, and John witnessed the miracle of the spiritual transformation of Jesus right before their very eyes, *"When his clothes became dazzling white, whiter than anyone in the world could bleach them."* (Mark 9:3). The amazement did not stop there. In Mark 9:7, *"a voice came from the cloud: "This is my Son, whom I love. Listen to him!""* It was God Himself validating the deity of Jesus. Just like any proud Jamaican father would say in our native language to others, "Ah my yout dat. Mi luv im, so mek sure oonuh lissen im."

God's expression of His love for His Son made me think of something my brother, Damien, said to me recently. He said our father, who passed away over thirty years ago—whose birthday incidentally was in February—must be so proud. When I asked him why, he reminded me that Daddy had once said he wished that one of us would go into ministry. I am not quite there, but I have had my own spiritual change, and I do like to proclaim the gospel, sometimes using words.

I recall some years ago going to the dentist, who was a family friend, for a simple filling, or so I thought. As soon as the dentist administered the local anaesthetic, I knew something was wrong. I had the presence of mind to tell him I was feeling strange. My breathing was laboured, and I felt like I was blacking out. The next thing I knew, I was hearing the doctor from what sounded like a mile away telling his assistant to alert the hospital, and he was bringing me in himself; don't even call an ambulance as that would take longer. I could sense when I was placed in a car. The dentist kept calling my name, poking me, and telling me not to go to sleep. In my mind, I kept repeating, "God, help me!" I am not sure when I got to the hospital, but I remember seeing lights. Apparently, it was the emergency room doctors shining their light into my eyes. I realised that I had had an allergic reaction to the anaesthetic, and the outcome could have been fatal. I decided to live in praise to God.

Yes, my friend. We can all have a transforming experience through Christ, not necessarily in a flash of light, but others will be able to see our spiritual change in how we live our lives. In addition, as a theme of our church says, "Disciples of Christ, hearing the call, walking with Jesus. One Love."

Reflection of Luke 8:40-56

In Sickness and in Health

The Gospel writer, Luke, was a physician by profession. So, it is not surprising that he chronicles many miracles of healing by Jesus, the Great Physician. Today, as we see so many cases of sickness around us, it serves as a reminder that Jesus is still working overtime. He is still our miracle worker, in sickness and in health.

The title for Luke 8:40-56 in some translations is *A Dead Girl and a Sick Woman.* It is a well-known one. It also appears in Matthew 9:18-26 and Mark 5:22-43. It means this was a significant event in the ministry of Jesus and that it resonated with the Gospel writers.

The passage also speaks of faith and healing. Two verses, in particular, zero in on the importance of faith. In Luke 8:48, Jesus tells the woman who touched His cloak and was healed after a long battle with her health that, *"Daughter, your faith has healed you. Go in peace."* This was also echoed in His words in Luke 8:50 to the desperate father of the child who was said to be dead, *"Don't be afraid; just believe, and she will be healed."* You see, my friend, faith is important in the miracle of healing the mind, body, or soul. Never lose hope, as through Christ, ALL things are possible.

Meris Haughton

The story shows us too that sickness is no respecter of age, station in life, or anything else for that matter. Think about it. The story tells of two very different people. One was sick for a short time, while the other was sick for twelve years. One was a girl, while the other was a woman. One was from a family of substance, while the other was broke. In our current time, we see many examples of sickness, especially during the COVID-19 pandemic. In Jamaica, it afflicted persons from one day old to one hundred and eight years old, males and females, politicians and constituents, rich man, poor man, beggar man, thief; all have been touched by the pandemic or other illnesses.

The common message in the story, and as it should be with all of us today, is to have faith. Yes, my friend, no matter what we are going through, we need to have faith.

I have witnessed the power of faith in my own family repeatedly. I remember in 2014, when my mom was diagnosed with stage four cancer. As you can imagine, this was a very stressful period for the family. However, through faith and the support of skilled surgeons, and the prayers of family and friends, she miraculously got better. For five wonderful years after, she lived her life and loved.

I saw the power of faith again when one of my aunts battled multiple myeloma. This is an illness with an average life expectancy after diagnosis of four years. My aunt was our family miracle. Thanks be to God, she lived for over eight years after her diagnosis. It was not an easy road, but she had such faith and showed such joy in the little things in life. She was as thankful for sunshine, as she was thankful for rain, thankful for joy, and thankful for pain, as they all reminded her that she was alive. You know how most people say, "Take it one day at a time." She used to say take life one minute at a time. This is true, as none of us knows when the roll will be called up yonder.

It was obvious she also believed in the biblical prescription for healing found in Proverbs 17:22, which says, *"A cheerful heart is good medicine, but a crushed spirit dries up the bones."* I am no doctor, but I also recommend this to you. You see, laughter is a prescription to stimulate health and healing. It gives us a positive perspective on life. It allows joy to fill our hearts. Laughter is a medicine that costs little and yields great results.

So, my friend, the moral of the story is that to heal the body, mind and soul, we should have faith. Blend that with some laughter and stir in the reality that we are never alone, and we will have the remedy.

Be encouraged by these words, *"When storms come your way, just remember you know the Master of the wind. When sickness finds you, remind yourself that you know the Great Physician. When your heart gets broken, just say 'I know the Potter.'"*

It does not matter what we are facing or going through, Jesus is the way, the truth, and the life. He is everything we need.

CHAPTER 8

BLESSINGS OF LIFE

"For from his fullness we have all received, grace upon grace." (John 1:16 – ESV).

Through the grace of God, we receive so many blessings. Sometimes it may not seem that way. However, if we were to count our blessings one by one, we would be amazed by God's grace in our lives.

God knows us and loves us. He provides all our needs according to His riches in glory (see Philippians 4:19). He blesses us and asks that we bless others as we are blessed.

Reflection of Luke 7:1-17

He Knows My Name

As I used the *Our Daily Bread* one morning as a devotional guide, I came across an interesting quote that read, "It's not what you know, it's who you know." Others would debatably say it is not who you know but who knows you.

Think about it, my friend. How many times have we heard stories about someone who is well qualified but cannot get a job because of where they live or they did not know someone in an influential position? But, then again, they could know the person, but the person does not know them like that, so they are not willing to recommend them for a job opportunity.

Of course, if we are talking about Jesus, both statements are true; it is who we know and who knows us. The two stories shared in Luke 7:1-17, although they are entirely different, are a perfect example of the premise of who we know and who knows us. Of course, the one common thread is Jesus.

Luke 7:1-10 is entitled, in some translations, **The Faith of the Centurion**. It recounts a Centurion, who, through his emissaries, appeals to Jesus to save his servant from afar, as he didn't think he was worthy of Jesus coming under his roof. You see, the Centurion obviously knew who Jesus was and believed in His miraculous power to heal by just speaking it into being. The story says, Jesus was amazed by the Centurion's faith.

In our time and in our lives, we need to recognise who Jesus is. If only we had such faith, we could move mountains.

In the second story in Luke 7:11-17, known as ***Jesus Raises a Widow's Son***, Jesus came upon a funeral procession. He knew who the widow was; He knew she had lost her one and only son; He knew the hardship she would face; He knew how much she was hurting. The text says He had compassion on her and raised him from the dead without even being asked.

My friend, Jesus knows us too. He knows our name. He knows our pain. To paraphrase the words of the popular song, *That's What Friends Are For*, He knows us in good times and bad times. He will be on our side forevermore. As a friend, that is what He is for.

Luke 7:1-17 shares two different stories, but one Jesus. What is also common to both stories is the love and compassion of Jesus. Therefore, whether you demonstrate faith like the Centurion and ask for Christ's help or if you do not even know how or what to ask like the Widow, Christ knows us, knows our needs, and dispenses His mercy and goodness equally.

So, my friend, have faith, yes, but all is not lost if we do not know what to ask. Additionally, take careful note of Luke 7:17 which reads, *"This news about Jesus spread throughout Judea and the surrounding country."* We should be sharing news about the goodness of God in our own lives. So, testify about your own experiences or those of others you know.

I also encourage you to show the same love and compassion that Christ showed. We do not have to wait for someone to ask for our help. If we see someone in need and we can do something to help him or her, just do it.

Remember, God's favour is based on grace, mercy, and compassion, not on works or favour. We should therefore have faith as seen in the first story, but it is clear from the second story that God grants mercy even when, in our blindness, we cannot or will not ask.

So, let us commit to grow in our trust in Jesus who has both infinite power and extraordinary compassion.

Let's pray:

> "Heavenly Father, I thank You for knowing my name, and for knowing what I want. I praise You for never changing; Your mercies are *'new every morning!'* (see Lamentations 3:23). Help us to look forward to what You have for us today and every day.

From the Pews

I declare that as long as I live, I will sing of the goodness of God."

Reflection of John 3:22-36

Testify of the Goodness of God

God is good all the time; all the time, God is good. I am sure that most, if not all, have said this at one time or another. It is something we say, sometimes without even thinking. It is such a simple way to testify of the goodness of God.

In some versions of the Bible, the passage in John 3:22-36 is entitled, ***John Testifies Again About Jesus***. In it, John testifies of the divinity and the goodness of God. Friend, I truly believe that we, in our time, should practice testifying about the goodness of God in our own lives. Moreover, even in the midst of challenges that sometimes seem overwhelming, there is so much goodness and blessings.

Personally, I am a firm believer in speaking about the goodness of Christ in my own life, even in the face of adversity. I recall one particular occasion when I had a difficult week. It started out before dawn one Sunday with a call from the older of my two brothers that he was at an emergency room. It turned out that he had a deep vein thrombosis, which, for us mere mortals, is a blood clot. This serious condition could easily have had a fatal outcome. You may ask, "So where is the goodness in that?" But, thanks be to God, it was caught early as he had the presence of mind to go to the ER. He was hospitalised for a few days.

The responses from the doctors, nurses, family, friends, and even neighbours were amazing, and, I truly believe, inspired by God. When my brother drove up to the hospital, he was not able to get out of the car. Thankfully, an orderly had noticed a car drive in but no one getting out. So, he went out and wheeled my brother in. The doctors and nurses immediately attended to him. After going to my brother's house to get his essentials, his neighbour was kind enough to drive me back to the hospital to retrieve my brother's car. Family and friends, including my church family, made sure I had support and prayers throughout the ordeal. I have to testify that God IS good.

What does the term "to testify" or "to give one's testimony" really mean? Christians use the term to mean telling the story of how one became a Christian. It also refers to a specific event in a person's life in which God transformed them or a situation that caused them to see the work of Jesus Christ in and through them.

Truthfully, I have faced many tough situations over the last few years. In fact, since 2009, my family has had a major crisis of death or serious illness every two years that sometimes make me feel like Job. Nevertheless, my friend, through Christ, and by the power of prayer and the fellowship of faith, I have always been lifted. No matter what, I still feel blessed. This is why I am a firm believer and will tell anyone who will listen that, through Christ, ALL things are possible.

Meris Haughton

Yes, my friend, testimony is a powerful tool for sharing what God has done and is continuing to do in our lives; every minute, every hour, every day. It is an opportunity for us to tell of the saving grace of Christ. Sharing our testimony can lead another person to believe in Christ, as was the purpose of John testifying about Christ to his disciples.

Apart from us following the example of John, in 1 Peter 3:15-16, God also invites us to share our testimony. It reads, *"Instead, you must worship Christ as Lord of your life. And if someone asks about your hope as a believer, always be ready to explain it. But do this in a gentle and respectful way. Keep your conscience clear. Then if people speak against you, they will be ashamed when they see what a good life you live because you belong to Christ."*

Friend, we must not only testify about the goodness of Christ in words but also in our deeds. How we live our lives should also be a testimony.

Therefore, as we journey through life, we must tell and show others the blessings on our lives. Let us pledge to make our light shine and light the way for others to come to Christ. Let us testify of our many stories about how God has worked in our lives. Let us use our testimonies to encourage others who may presently be going through a similar situation. Let them see in us the hope that they long to have. Let them taste and see that God is always faithful. Let us forever sing of the goodness of God.

Reflection of Luke 13:31-35

Serving Others is a Blessing

"Blessed is he who comes in the name of the Lord." (Luke 13:35).

In some translations, this passage is entitled ***Jesus' Sorrow For Jerusalem***. With all the ills happening on our island, we could say ***Jesus' Sorrow For Jamaica***. As I prepared for this reflection, I remembered that in Christ there is hope. I was therefore inspired to focus on service. Interestingly, the *Our Daily Bread* always has *service* as one of the main topics. I guess service is a timeless subject.

As Christians, we are all called to serve. But do we all answer that call? Sadly, the answer is no. Nevertheless, serving others is a noble cause. It is something that we should do intentionally as we follow the example set by Christ. If you think about it, at some time or another, we all want to be served. So, why not practice the golden rule that we learnt that is written in Matthew 7:12, *"So in everything, do to others what you would have them do to you, for this sums up the Law and the Prophets."*

Our service should not be self-serving, as it is not about us. I remember hearing stories of a former politician who would not even speak to a group of constituents unless a TV crew was present. I guess he felt that if the media did not cover it, then no one would know he was serving the people.

Seriously, friend, our good works should be self-sacrificing. It should not matter if anyone knows. In fact, Matthew 6:1 exhorts us to *"Be careful not to practice your 'acts of righteousness' in front of others to be seen by them. If you do, you will have no reward from your Father in heaven."* I know many persons who take this quite seriously. They quietly support causes, donate to others, and do not want their good deeds reported publicly.

Remember, my friend, no service is too small. In Matthew 10:42, Jesus said, *"If anyone gives even a cup of cold water... he will certainly not lose his reward.*" Therefore, do what you can to help the poor, sick, lonely, distressed, and hungry; those vulnerable and marginalized in any way.

Remember that service is not servitude and therefore should not be seen as demeaning. In fact, we would be in good company as the Master Himself washed the feet of His disciples. I often see my pastor doing that humble act on a Holy Thursday when he, too, as a reminder of Jesus' act of love for His disciples, washes the feet of some congregants.

A sad reality though is that some we have tried to serve have actually turned against us or, as my mother of blessed memory—who liked to use Jamaican proverbs—often said, "Sorry fi mawga dawg, mawga dawg tun roun' bite yuh." This means, you may help a person in need who ends up harming you in return for your kindness. Sadly, this has happened to me on several occasions. A beggar has even threatened me, right in church, the one time I did not have any change or food to give him.

But, friend, we should not let that stop us from doing what God calls us to do, and what Jesus lamented about in Luke 13:34 when He said, *"How often I have longed to gather your children together, as a hen gathers her chicks under her wings, and you were not willing."* We still have to continue His mission to love and serve one another, and to spread the good news of God.

Therefore, my friend, like Jesus, we should remain resolute in serving God. So, do not let anything or anyone get in the way of you doing good deeds. I mean, we may not be driving out demons and healing people, but today, tomorrow, and every day, we should continue to serve in whatever way we can, in spite of the personal costs. Our goal is to serve each other and, more importantly, serve God.

As the Apostle Paul urges us to do, let us display the fruit of the Spirit in our lives, to "serve one another humbly in love" and to demonstrate "kindness" and "goodness." Therefore, friend, let us look at how we can all intentionally love and serve our neighbours and demonstrate the fruit of the Spirit in the way we treat others.

I challenge us to look for opportunities to help someone. It does not only have to be about giving money. It could be going through your closet and donating those clothes and shoes that can no longer fit you or you no longer wear; those in good condition, of course. It could be spending a little time talking to or shopping for an elderly person in your community. It could be donating food packages to needy persons in your neighbourhood. There are so many things that we can do and so many ways we can serve others.

I pray: *"Lord, help me; help us to serve others out of love for You. Through our deeds, fan the flame of service in others."*

I want to share a quote the Pope shared in a sermon in Cuba. He said, *"Whoever does not live to serve, does not 'serve' to live."*

Reflection of John 7:14-36

We Are God's Messengers

In John 7:16, there is a suggestion that we can all be messengers. A few years ago, if someone had said to me that you would become one of God's messengers, I would have called them crazy. You see, friend, none of us knows what tomorrow will bring or where God will lead us in this life. I mean, who would have thought that today, my life's journey would be on this particular path of sharing meditations in worship or writing a book.

It was at the height of the COVID-19 pandemic that the Church of St. Margaret, Liguanea, introduced Evening Prayers. It was a daily moment of calm that began out of the chaos of COVID-19. It is a mission that started with a core of just three persons, which, thanks be to God, over a two-year period, has grown to a roster of about fifteen regular messengers. I feel blessed that I am now one of these messengers who, on first Fridays, share thoughts through brief reflections.

It feels like it was just yesterday that my pastor first invited me to lead and share a reflection. Truthfully, when he asked me, I wondered if he was clothed in his right mind. You see, I have not been to a theological seminary like him; I am not a lay leader; neither am I an evangelist. I am but an ordinary person. He must have seen something in me that I did not see in myself.

Meris Haughton

I imagine that must be how Moses felt when God commanded him to speak to Pharaoh to let the Israelites out of bondage. Exodus 4:10-11 reminds us that, "Who the Lord calls, He equips." I had no challenges speaking to an audience, as I do that all the time, but never about the Bible or religion. This was completely out of my comfort zone. But when you think about it, I am not alone. The Bible, as well as life as we know it, has many stories of ordinary people being called or feeling led to share a message or a testimony of Christ. But, like everything in life, we should pray to God for guidance. Therefore, I prayed about that first meditation I was to do in June 2020, and a voice inside me said, "Meris, why are you anxious? Just do it. You'll be fine." I did it, and I was fine. Surprisingly, it was such a rewarding experience. So, here I am, years later, still sharing.

In fact, every time, as I prepare to share a reflection, I remember Psalm 19:14, *"Let the words of my mouth, and the meditation of my heart, be acceptable in thy sight, O Lord, my strength and redeemer."* Friend, sometimes the message comes at some odd times. I could be gardening, resting, having a conversation, being in church, a meeting, or even sitting on the proverbial throne, and a word comes to me.

Serving in this way has allowed me, as it can also allow you, to deepen our Christian commitment. For me, in preparing to share, I have had to read the appointed scripture with an open heart and mind, often using different versions of the Bible. It is so amazing that you can see the passages from different perspectives, even those stories that are so familiar from those days in Sunday School.

What I did not bargain for was the blessing the feedback from others has brought me when they shared how the messages have blessed them. My Aunt Patsy, who passed away in 2022, used to tell me how the messages lifted her spirit while she battled her health challenges. Some have even said that they have used these messages in their own personal devotions or shared them with others. The glory is to God, not me. To God be the glory great things He has done. It is why I can relate to John 7:16, which says, *"My teaching is not my own. It comes from the one who sent me."* You see, my thoughts shared over the past few years are really messages from God. I am merely the channel.

I have answered the call and have since committed to leading on the first Friday of each month. I also do so on special occasions, like on my birthday or whenever I am asked, and I am able to. In addition, as I get older and hopefully wiser, I pray that the Lord continues to use me. If I can reach even one person, I feel blessed.

I invite you to be still, listen, and answer the call of God to serve in this or any other way, as I truly believe we all have a message within us. Therefore, I encourage others, whether they are young or just older youths, who feel led to share the word, just do it, even once. Take it from me, God will enable you too. Yes, friend, as Christ commanded in Matthew 28:19-20, we are called to be part of the great commissioning to spread the news of the goodness of God.

Therefore, my friend, share your messages and testimonies in words or by your deeds. Let our actions tell the good news of Christ, just as our words do.

Reflection of Matthew 27:55-66

The Ministrations of Women

From Genesis to Revelation, we see several women featured in scripture. It is the same throughout history. The world has been blessed with the good works of global figures like Mother Theresa, Florence Nightingale, my church's patron saint, Queen Margaret of Scotland, and our very own British-Jamaican nurse, Mary Seacole, who all ministered to the spiritual and physical needs of so many.

Moreover, as a proud graduate of Alpha Academy, an all-girl Catholic school in Kingston, Jamaica, I have to mention the inspirational role of Jesse Ripoll, who founded the noble institution. Some of the women of my time are the renowned Sister Mary Bernadette Little of blessed memory, all the Sisters of Mercy, and hundreds of noted women of excellence who carry on the legacy of my alma mater.

As we see in Matthew 27:55-66, women were also part of Jesus' circle, taking care of the needs of the disciples. Matthew 27:55 says, *"Many women were there, watching from a distance. They had followed Jesus from Galilee to care for his needs."* You see, friend, although Jesus and the disciples are the central figures of the New Testament, women played an important role in catering to their needs.

This allowed Jesus to focus on His ministry. Of course, as women, we are often the practical and nurturing ones.

These same women were committed to their support for Christ, even in death. As Jesus was hurriedly buried on the eve of the Sabbath, the scripture tells us that the women watched and waited. Matthew 27:61 says, *"Mary Magdalene and the other Mary were sitting there opposite the tomb."* For their faithful ministrations, their reward was being the first ones to see the risen Christ on Resurrection Sunday.

Today, women continue to play a vital role in ministry. In our Anglican Diocese, we have church organizations like the Altar Guild that prepares the altar for worship, and the Women's Auxiliary and the Mother's Union that both focus on ministering to the needs of the church, families and others. It is this same sense of empathy and service that allow women to dominate professions like nursing, teaching, and caregiving, which are all service-oriented and Christian ministrations. Women also now spread the word, serving as evangelists, deaconesses, priests, and even bishops.

Whether you are woman, man, or child, we are all created in the image of God. I therefore encourage our women especially to continue to give service to the church and the needy; individually and collectively. As Christ said to His disciples in Matthew 9:37, *"The harvest is plentiful, but the labourers are few."* Matthew 9:38 implores us to *"Ask the Lord of the harvest to send out labourers into his harvest."*

Meris Haughton

Reflection of Matthew 9:9-17

I Will Follow Him

Jesus' invitation to Matthew in Matthew 9:9 was two simple but powerful words, *"Follow Me."* The response was simply divine intervention as Matthew's heart was touched, and he *"got up and followed Him."*

Every time I think of those words and the calling of Matthew, I think of the song made popular by the movie *Sister Act*, "I will follow Him." I often find myself singing it, even though I cannot carry a tune.

The Calling of Matthew is an episode in the life of Jesus that appears in all three synoptic gospels (Matthew 9:9–13, Mark 2:13–17 , and Luke 5:27–28). But my reflection is based on the gospel of Matthew. It relates to the initial encounter between Jesus and Matthew, a tax collector. Tax collectors, in biblical times, were considered traitors and sinners. The religious leaders of the time objected to Jesus associating with Matthew and his friends. However, in Jesus' own words, *"I have not come to call the righteous but sinners." (Mark 9:13)*. Therefore, Matthew answered the call and followed Jesus, eventually becoming an apostle.

Matthew walked away from his lucrative job as a tax collector to follow Jesus. I am not sure that, as a practising tax administrator, I could do that. However, I do not think

Jesus is asking any of us to leave our jobs. What He is asking us to do is leave behind the things that go against His teachings: those malpractices like lying, cheating, stealing, sexual immorality, gossiping, covetousness, being judgmental, or having negative feelings like hate, envy, pity, self-righteousness. He desires for us to follow His way of truth and light, to love God and love our neighbours.

An aspect of following Christ is for us to share the good news of our blessings with our own family, friends, and all we meet, so they too can experience God's saving grace. This is what Matthew did when he shared a dinner with not just Jesus and His disciples but had also invited his friends and colleagues to join (see Matthew 9:10). Matthew saw it as important to share Christ with his friends and colleagues. We also need to reach out to others wherever they are and share Christ with them.

Not everyone agrees that as a follower of Christ, we should associate with those we consider sinners. Like the Pharisees of biblical times, who asked the disciples, *"Why does your teacher eat with tax collectors and sinners?" (see Matthew 9:11)*, we still have persons asking that question today. They seem to have omitted the part of the Bible that says in Matthew 7:1, *"Do not judge, or you too will be judged."*

It reminds me of a controversy a few years ago in Jamaica, when, for the first time, a gospel artiste dared to perform on a major reggae and dancehall stage show. For weeks, the religious community and all the radio and television discussion programs debated the pros and cons. The simple response of the artiste and his pastor, who fully supported him, was that he wanted to bring his message of Christ outside of the church. This is exactly what Jesus meant in Matthew 9:12 when He said, *"It is not the healthy who need a doctor, but the sick."*

Let me remind you, as I often remind myself, that we are all sinners; no exception. None of us is perfect. None of us is better than anyone else. However, thank God for His saving grace and for inviting us to follow Him.

Friend, just as Jesus called Matthew to follow Him, He calls us today. Let us do as Matthew did and answer the call. Our walk with Jesus can be as transforming for us as it was for Matthew. The influence of Jesus was so far-reaching that even today, Matthew is the patron saint of tax collectors and accountants. I am not suggesting that you walk away from your job, but we should leave behind whatever is making us stumble on life's road.

Like Matthew, we should share the good news of Jesus with our colleagues, families, friends, and our universal neighbours, and invite them to follow Him too.

Let us remember that by following Jesus, Matthew was a witness of Jesus' ascension and continued in ministry even after. We too are blessed to continue in Christ's ministry by proclaiming and living the Word.

Yes, sometimes we will face the storms of life, we will have mountains of challenges to climb, we will feel like we are drowning in an ocean, but, friend, just follow Jesus. He will lead us home.

Like the words of the song says, which should be our theme song, "I will follow Him. Ever since He touched my heart, I knew there isn't an ocean too deep; a mountain so high it can keep, keep me away, away from His love. I love Him and where He goes, I'll follow."

ABOUT THE AUTHOR

Meris Haughton is a well-known Jamaican Tax Administrator and government communicator dubbed the "Tax Lady" in her profession, but her passion is for Christ. She is a woman of faith who sees God in everything around her. She has always lived her life helping others. She enjoys sharing her experiences to encourage and motivate others through her speaking and writing. Next to her faith is the love of her family, who are proud of their Jamaican heritage. Meris believes that her purpose is to strengthen others through her words and deeds.

www.ingramcontent.com/pod-product-compliance
Lightning Source LLC
Chambersburg PA
CBHW070455100426
42743CB00010B/1636